God as Śūnya

Dr Tandra Patnaik

11 September 1947 – 11 May 2015

God as Śūnya

The Philosophy of Mahimā Dharma and Bhīmā Bhoi

Tandra Patnaik

PRINTWORLD
Publishers of Indian Traditions

Cataloging in Publication Data – DK

[Courtesy: D.K. Agencies (P) Ltd. <docinfo@dkagencies.com>]

Patnaik, Tandra, author.

God as śūnya : the philosophy of Mahimā Dharma and Bhīmā Bhoi / Tandra Patnaik.

pages cm

Includes bibliographical references (pages).

ISBN: 9788124608319

1. God (Hinduism) 2. Sunyata. 3. Mahima Dharma. 4. Hindu philosophy. 5. Bhima Bhoi, 1852-1895–Philosophy. I. Title.

DDC 294.5211 23

ISBN: 978-81-246-0831-9

First published in India, 2016

Printed and published by:

D.K. Printworld (P) Ltd.

Regd. Office: *Vedaśrī*, F-395, Sudarshan Park

(Metro Station: Ramesh Nagar), New Delhi – 110 015

Phones: (011) 2545 3975, 2546 6019; *Fax*: (011) 2546 5926

e-mail: indology@dkprintworld.com

Website: www.dkprintworld.com

To

Lord Jagannātha
for His kind blessings
to complete this work

Endless are the agonies and sorrows of living.
Who can bear to witness?
Condemn my life to hell
But let the world be redeemed.

— **Bhīmā Bhoi,**
Stuti-Cintamaṇi, 27.7

Prologue

When my mother sent the manuscript of *God as Śūnya* to Susheel-ji of D.K. Printworld on 1 January 2015, she probably knew that she would never see it come out as a book. During the final proof-reading of the book, a task that finally came to me in her absence, I came across a draft letter to Susheel-ji while searching among her handwritten notes and references. In it she thanked Lord Jagannātha for permitting her to complete the book, but she also shared her misgivings about what would happen in the future due to her deteriorating health. Her premonitions, unfortunately, proved to be true. On 11 May 2015 she breathed her last. But in some sense, her labour in this world was over. She left no incomplete work, whether academic, social or domestic. She told us what to do and not to do with our lives. And she bore her dying with grace. Two days before she passed away, Susheel-ji called to say that he was sending the manuscript for final corrections. I communicated the same to her. She only smiled with satisfaction and nodded – she knew that her work was done and that Susheel-ji and I would see to the rest of it. For her, I felt then, it was as if the book had already come out.

I have tried my best to proof-read the book well and to take care of most of the errors and incomplete references. Susheel-ji and D.K. Printworld have done a wonderful job of bringing out a superb production and we hope that this last work of my mother on the Oḍiyā philosophical tradition convinces all of the rich heritage of Odisha much of which is yet to be discovered.

Priyadarshi Patnaik

Preface

WHAT attracted me to the philosophy of Mahimā Dharma was its remarkable stance towards religion, man and society. Though a part of the Indian religio-philosophical tradition, the boldness with which it defies idolatry, meaningless rites, religious pomposities and above all, rejects the shameful practice of social discrimination on the basis of *varṇa dharma/jāti,* leaves one mesmerized. When I poured into its literature composed by Bhīmā Bhoi, I realized that it has much more depth than I had imagined. Bhīmā Bhoi not only presents a *śūnya*-centric metaphysics but does not hesitate to take it to its logical conclusion. Though the idea of God as *śūnya* is not exactly an unknown idea in Indian philosophical tradition, one marks a certain amount of compromise as far as its affliation to some sectarian God is concerned. It is either Śiva or Viṣṇu or the Buddhist deity Vajrasattva. But in case of Mahimā Dharma there is no trace of compromise either in its attitude to God or to the society. What is likely to amaze us is that Bhīmā Bhoi, the chief protagonist of this *dharma,* was just an illiterate tribal young man who neither had access to the classical texts nor to the literature of the medieval *sant*s of Odisha. Yet the ease with which he presents through his lyrical compositions very rarefied concepts like the idea of *Śūnya-Brahman,* the idea of the identity between *jīva* and *Brahman,* or for that matter the relation between the cosmic body (*brahmāṇḍa*) and individual body (*piṇḍa*), the concept *bhakti* as *ātmajñāna* leaves one awe-struck. It is a fact that Bhīmā Bhoi's style of presentation, choice of philosophical ideas and words bear a clear stamp of his predecessors of Odisha, especially Pañcasakhā and Caitanya Dāsa. Still it would be an injustice on our part to say that after almost a gap of more than two centuries he replicated those ideas. Probably, the *śūnya*-centric philosophy and all the allied concepts had become a part of the collective psyche of the common mass of the soil. Bhīmā Bhoi perhaps starts from here and sails to its logical conclusion that any *śūnya*-centric metaphysics in India, including the preceding Utkalīya Vaiṣṇavism, could have reached. He does not present his ideas in a half-hearted manner and there is not an iota of conciliation at any step. Woking on the path-breaking philosophical ideas of Mahimā Dharma, for me, was an exhilirating experience.

Throughout the book I have used "Odisha" and "Odia" instead of "Orissa" and "Oriya" since the rendering of the change of nomenclature was accepted by Government of India on 4 November 2011.

The work on the project was undertaken as a Senior Fellow of the Indian Council of Philosophical Research (ICPR). I am grateful to the Council for offering me the Fellowship. On this occasion I would like to fondly remember Avadhuta Nityananda Baba of Mahimā Gādī, Dhenkanal and Avadhuta Nishakar Baba of Mahimā Ashram, Bomikhal, Bhubaneswar for sharing their knowledge with me. I would like to express my heart-felt gratitude to Sri Sadananda Agarwal, the famous Mahimā scholar and a great organizer, who offered me chance to spend time at Khaliapali Ashrama of Bhīmā Bhoi. I am equally indebted to my family members for encouraging me to edit and fine-tune the work. My sincere thanks to D.K. Printworld for readily accepting this work for publishing.

1 April 2015 **Tandra Patnaik**

Contents

1

Introduction

I. Dhama and Darśana: Paradoxes and Anomalies

THE very title of this book may raise many eyebrows. I am likely to be assailed by the academic philosophers on two counts. First, can there be a conception of God who is of the nature of *śūnya* (the word has been often translated as "void" or "emptiness")? Second, can a subject matter called philosophy include the concept *dharma* within its fold? In this introductory note I would like to address these two questions. Surprisingly there are many existing anomalies, especially, regarding the second question, that needs to be sorted out before I handle the central theme of my book.

Many of my friends, even from the academic circle, have raised serious doubts about the possibility of the idea of God as *śūnya*, even if *śūnya* means not "void", but the God as a formless, non-categorizable principle. They have often argued that this may be possible as a lofty speculation but it lacks practical applicability. I assure them that the idea of *śūnya* as God is not so strange to our philosophical and religious tradition. Right from such orthodox Brāhmanical traditions like Kashmir Śaivism, Vīraśaivism and Odishan Vaiṣṇavism to such non-Brāhmanical schools like Tantric Buddhism have delineated God as *śūnya*. As far as the practicality of such a concept is concerned I can vouchsafe from my personal experience that there are still some religio-philosophical orders like Mahimā Dharma which staunchly hold to the view that God can be nothing more than *Śūnya-Brahma* – God without form and figure, even without a symbolic representation. They still stand under the open sky morning and evening and pray for the well-being of the whole humanity. I shall not dwell here longer on the issue since my work aims to unravel the philosophical structure of a *dharma* that truly adheres to the principle of God as *śūnya*. So now I would like to address the second issue that is much more complicated. This is about the question of discussing the philosophy of a *dharma*. This may sound quite anomalous as we are given to believe that the word *dharma* is "God-centric"; so talking of the philosophy of a *dharma* is like putting a circle in a square hole. But I am convinced that both the terms "philosophy" and "*dharma*" are taken in most cases in the narrowest sense of the terms. Though academic scholars have filled pages on clarifying that *dharma* does not necessarily mean religion – their personal conviction that *dharma* is nothing more than religion (not even spirituality) is so overpowering that they do not want to touch anything that is remotely associated with the term as a subject matter of academic investigation. But if we adopt this logic, then we should not use the word *dharma* in case of Buddhism and Jainism, for there is no place for God in both the philosophical movements. If the very conception of God makes philosophy a *dharma* then any system of accredited philosophy that conceives of God as the highest reality should not have been called a *darśana*, by the same logic. If systems like Nyāya, Yoga and Viśiṣṭādvaitavāda are not identified as *dharma* but *darśana*s despite presupposing the existence of God, then would not it be unjust on our part to have reservations about appending the word *darśana* to such lofty philosophical ideas championed by the *nirguṇa-panthī*s like Kabīr, Lal Dêd or Odishan Vaiṣṇavas and Mahimā-dharmīs? None of them talks of God in the personal sense. All these so-called dharmic positions are founded on strong metaphysical principles like any accredited philosophical system of the Classical age. They too have their own views about the nature of reality, the nature of truth, the nature of *mokṣa* as well the relation between the phenomenal and transcendental reality. I have so far not come across any clear argument that could offer the rationale behind such anomalous attitude.

Is it because the powerful orthodox and elitist elements have felt threatened by any philosophical stream of thought that influenced the life of the ordinary people? For example, in the initial phases of Buddhism it was identified as *dharma*. No doubt during that phase the term *dharma* had not acquired a conspicuous religious connotation. May be because Buddha preached his thought in Pāli language (which was the language of the common people) and common folks were attracted by the teachings of the Buddha, the orthodox section wanted to sideline this popular mode of doing philosophy by bracketing it as *dharma,* i.e. a "movement" or a distinct "way of life". It is an irony that when Buddhism in later phases was subdivided into multiple systems and when the trend of composing their texts in the form of Kārikās, Sūtras and Bhāṣyas became a part of their writings they acquired the status of *darśana*, for example, Mādhyamika *darśana* or Yogācāra *darśana*. So it seems that the elitist dogma that Sanskrit is the only language of doing philosophy (being the language of gods or *devabhāṣā*) and writing in the form of Kārikās and Sūtras is the only parameter of judging a philosophical treatise continued unabated. Anything that deviated from the practice was segregated as the "other".

It remains a hard fact that academic philosophers show little interest in investigating the continuation of the Indian philosophical tradition beyond the Classical age. Though philosophical ideas came pouring in from different parts of India in the form of distinct regional movements the post-Classical philosophy in India continues to remain in oblivion. By "post-Classical" I mean the philosophical developments after thirteenth century CE. The reason for such hesitation is not very difficult to trace. Such philosophical traditions are most often set aside as *panthas* (sects) or *dharma* (as in case of Sikh Dharma and Mahimā Dharma). During the post-Classical period the Indian philosophical tradition (which the post-colonial scholars prefer to brand as "Bhakti movement") found expression more in the form of movements than systems of thought. The pure intellectual speculation of classical tradition like Sāṁkhya or Vedānta was replaced by lived philosophies closer to society and life. The new way of doing philosophy, may be due to the reason stated above, has been put under the label *dharma*. The word *darśana* is seldom used. For example, instead of Vaiṣṇava *darśana* the word

Vaiṣṇava Dharma is preferred. Does that mean that Vaiṣṇavism was not based on any philosophical structure? I do not think so, for, the philosophical foundation of Vaiṣṇavism was laid by post-Śaṅkara Vedāntins. What is the rationale behind such a change of nomenclature is a matter of serious investigation.

Is Bhakti Movement God-centric?

One of the most important reasons for the injustice meted out to the so-called Santhic or Dharmic tradition may lie with word *bhakti* which is often associated with the philosophical movements of the post-Classical phase. The thinkers of this period never identified themselves as *bhakti* theorists. It was a label tagged to it during the colonial and post-colonial period. Due to some unfathomable reason all these movements are brought under the omnibus *bhakti*. Unfortunately, the word *bhakti* is so intimately associated with religion that the academic philosophers tend to think that the post-Classical philosophy as a whole is nothing more than dogmatic religious outpourings. Yet these same scholars do not mind appending the word *darśana* to the theories of later Vedāntic philosophies advanced by Vallabha, Madhva or Nimbārka. All these systems of thought dwell in detail on the concept of *bhakti*. The only visible difference between the analysis of *bhakti* in the post-Classical phase and the later Vedāntins is that all these thinkers were *ācārya*s (drawn from the community of brāhmaṇas) and they wrote in the form of Bhāṣyas. No modern scholars would dare to set their philosophy aside as a form of Bhakti movement. It is unfortunate that the scholars seldom delve into the dynamics of the word *bhakti*. It is almost taken for granted that the word *bhakti* connotes a single meaning, viz. emotional attachment to a personalized Supreme Being. It is seldom noted that in Indian tradition in certain cases the concept of *bhakti* has been very significantly used without the postulation of a personal God. It may also stand for a path of knowledge that helps one to understand one's inner potentialities. For example, Śaṅkarācārya defines *bhakti* as an investigation into one's own being (*sva svarūpānusandhāna*). In the post-Classical phase there prevailed many systems of thought that interpreted *bhakti* in consonance with Śaṅkara's definition of the term, i.e. as a form of direct knowledge or else a form of realization of the highest truth through yogic methods. So the inclusion of the concept of *bhakti* does not necessarily prohibit the new systems of the post-Classical phase to have the status of *darśana*. Rather the theories advanced by this group of post-Classical philosophers helped the common and ordinary people to have a taste of spirituality that was so far denied to them by the dominant and powerful section of the society.

The Philosopher vis-à-vis the Mystic

Another anomaly that is more appalling is the use of the label "mysticism" by the post-colonial scholars to the high-level philosophical works of the personalities like Kabīr, Ezuthachan, Dādū, Lal Dêd, Mahimā-dharmīs and others. The word is borrowed by the modern scholars from the West. The misconception about the philosophy-worthiness of medieval Indian philosophical tradition comes from this word "mystic" that is profusely and I must say mindlessly used in case of the protagonists of the medieval philosophical thoughts. For understanding the root of the problem let us again look at the use of the word mysticism in the Western context. The word "mysticism" is a European word with a definite history. Most of the European writers have used it to denote an intuitive or ecstatic union with the deity, through contemplation, communion or other mental experiences, or to denote the potential union of the human soul with the ultimate reality. The term was used by the Western theologians to refer to the position upheld by the pseduo-Dionysius, like Meister Eckhart (1260–1328) because they interpreted it as a form of theology that talked of the union of the soul with the Godhead. The position is taken to be anti-Semitic. The dominant Christian tradition criticized Eckhart for introducing a form of pantheism that goes against basic tenets of Christianity. So they applied the epithet "mysticism" to such a distinct religious position. Thus the European religion used the word "mysticism" to set aside the high philosophical speculation of Eckhart and others from the scope of religion. Is it not an irony that the Indian philosophical tradition since its inception, especially the Upaniṣadic period, is based on this presupposition. Many of our philosophical traditions including the Advaita Vedānta are largely based on the principle – "All is one; and one is all; and ultimately this One transcends all categorical and conceptual discriminations." If this is mysticism, then we have nothing to be ashamed of it. This philosophical position is highly admired even today. Such a presupposition has never implied an abrasive form of religious belief. So it still remains unexplained why our English educated scholars love to use the word "mystic" with reference to such great original thinkers like Kabīr, Dādū or Bhīmā Bhoi instead of the word "philosopher".[1] It is intellectually and logically jarring to note that our Indian academicians use the logic of European religious order to exclude pure philosophy of the medieval phase from the scope of philosophy proper. Is it the hangover from colonialism or the so-called Orientalism which our scholars follow to very cunningly portray anything that does not fit in within their accepted norm as the "other". It may be frustrating to note that even in judging the Indian philosophy as wholesome Western scholars freely use the word "mysticism".[2] Indian scholars blindly following the usage (of course selectively), and mindlessly employ this term. What is still more puzzling is the double standard the Indian academic community uses to judge the rich and powerful philosophy of

[1] For example, *Devotinal Poets and Mystics*, New Delhi: Publication Division, Ministry of Information and Broadcasting, 1991; B. Baumer and J. Beltz (eds.), 2008, *Bhīmā Bhoi, Verses from the Void: Mystic Poetry of a Oriya Saint*, New Delhi: Manohar.

[2] Here W.T. Stace's blanket remark about Indian philosophy is worth-noting. He says philosophy in India is "passing out of a realm of thought, reason and philosophy into the dream and shadow land . . . mysticism, where the heavy scent of beautiful poison flower drugs the intellect and obliterates thought in a blissful langorous repose." (*A Critical History of Greek Philosophy*, 1982, p. 371.) Ironically, Stace makes such quotable remark that also includes Plato's mystical interpretation of the highest Reality, i.e. his theory of Idea. Unfortunately, our post-colonial scholars reserve this epithet for the post-Classical philosophy to caste it aside as the "other".

the age. While no sane scholar of India would dare to address Śaṅkarācārya as a mystic or his philosophy of non-dualism as a specimen of mysticism, they do not mind setting aside the similar philosophical contents of post-Classical thinkers as mysticism. Is it not an irony that most often the scholars forget that Śaṅkarācārya subscribes to a theory of soteriology and talks of *moksa* and *mukti*, which according to the Oriental norm would at best be a form of mysticism? Why this double standard? The only possible difference one can point out between the philosophy of the Classical phase (that includes Śaṅkarācārya) and the post-Classical phase is the use of language (Sanskrit) and the mode of expression (*bhāṣya*). The post-Classical thinkers did not use Sanskrit but regional language. They spoke their philosophy through simple and accessible poetry. Can we call this a ground rational enough to arbitrarily put them under the category of "mystics" rather than philosophers? Have not our post-colonial intellectuals used a double standard in judging the post-Classical philosophy? What is more painful is that such great thinkers as Kabīr, Bhīmā Bhoi and others are more known as mystic "poets" than as philosophers. In the process they have pushed back such powerful thinkers to the status of litterateurs rather than philosophers. Naturally most of the works done on such great *sants* as Kabīr, Ravidāss, Dādū, Jñāneśwar, Narsī Mehtā, or the Odia *sants* like Pañcasakhā and Mahimā protagonist like Bhīmā Bhoi are undertaken by the scholars of literature rather than philosophy. Therefore, we rarely come across such titles as "Philosophy of Kabīr" or "Philosophy of Ravidass". It is somehow, reassuring to note that during the last three decades scholars have broken the shackle of the prevalent dogma; and a number of serious works on the metaphysics of the Sikh Dharma have been published.[3]

The Tradition and Its Critique

At this point, however, I must attempt to set the records straight. It is a fact that philosophical thinking underwent some radical changes in

---

[3] Sashibala, 1999, Sikh Metaphysics; Nikky-Guninder Kaur Singh, 1981, *Physics and Metaphysics of the Guru Granth Sahib*, New Delhi: Sterling.

the post-Classical age. The unique feature of this genre of philosophy is the unprecedented shift from elitism to egalitarianism. For quite a long time philosophy (*darśana*) was considered to be matter of pure intellectual deliberation. Even soteriology that formed a part of the Classical Indian philosophy seldom had anything to do with the society. No wonder *darśana* was called Guhya-Śāstra (a deep and secret science) accessible to a few elites. What is more surprising is that a huge gap existed between the philosophy of life and the actual life. To prove my point here I take two prominent examples. First, according to Upaniṣadic and Advaita *darśana* there is non-duality and non-distinction between the *jīva* and *Brahman* (*aham brahmāsmi*). So logically it follows that each individual soul is divine and as far as divinity is concerned every conscious being has the same status. But when we come to its practical ramification in the societal level even the most broad-minded Advaitin made a severe discrimination between the pure and polluted people. Here one may be reminded of the famous anecdote of the encounter between Śaṅkarācārya and a *cāṇḍāla*.[4] Similarly, the Sāṁkhya philosophy

---

[4] The anecdote of Śaṅkarācārya's encounter with a *caṇḍāla* on the bank of the River Gaṅgā at Varanasi is quite illuminating. According to the anecdote once he went to take bath in River Gaṅgā. On his way back he encountered a *cāṇḍāla* with his dogs. As *cāṇḍāla* belongs to the caste of untouchables he was asked by Śaṅkarācārya to move away from his path. The *cāṇḍāla* did not move but in response asked, "Sir, you are expounding non-dualism but your action is contrary. You think that contact with my body will make you impure. But both these bodies – yours and mine are composed of the same five elements. If you are talking about the soul then the *ātman* in both of us is identical. So why do you ask me to get away from your path?" Śaṅkarācārya was stunned by the *cāṇḍāla*'s reply and realizing that such differentiation is false, composed the verse with five stanzas known as "Mānasa Pañcakam". The refrain at the end of each verse is – "One who looks at the creation from non-dualistic standpoint is a true teacher, be he a brāhmaṇa or *cāṇḍāla*." But still the question remains, even if a man is not as knowledgable as the *cāṇḍāla* should he be discriminated just because he happened to be born in the family of a *cāṇḍāla*?

holds that out of the two realities (*prakṛti* and *puruṣa*) *puruṣa* is the principle that stands for pure consciousness and the spirit. *Puruṣa* is plural in number as it is reflected as the pure spirituality in each individual soul. Obviously such a metaphysical stand implies that each individual soul reflects the qualities of *puruṣa*. So in the societal and practical level the theory should have implied the equality of each and one as far as inner spirituality is concerned. But perhaps none of the protagonists of such high philosophical speculation ever questioned the strict *varṇa-vyavasthā* (stratification of society on the basis of birth). None of these systems of thought ever bothered to highlight how the highest goal (*mokṣa*/*apavarga*) could be achieved by every member of the human society. So we find that the philosophical traditions in India, though they spoke about the plight of human beings in the *saṁsāra* and path to liberation, were only a matter of intellectual deliberation having virtually no link with the societal reality. With the advent of the post-Classical age the nature of philosophical deliberation underwent a drastic change. The yawning gap between the theory and practice was removed. Whether philosophical theories of this genre were non-dualistic or dualistic the door for self-realization was open to one and all. It was more inclusive that responded more to the spiritual needs of the common man. The theories propagated by these thinkers were more straightforward and less scholastic. As the targeted audience was not the *puṇḍit*s or the elites but the common mass, the medium of expression was the vernacular language, not Sanskrit. Lyrical poetry was most often used to substantiate the philosophical position rather than the Kārikās and Śūtras, which were commonly used in the philosophical treatises of the Classical age.

The most remarkable trait of this new line of thought was a deep sense of "non-conformism". It provided a critique of the tradition without crossing its limits. The fundamental philosophical theories like the law of *karma*, the cycle of rebirth, the basic theories of soteriology like *mokṣa* or *mukti* continued to be its basic presumptions. The philosophical speculations were targeted for the common folks, his life, his social ambience, his need for spiritual fulfilment. With an unprecedented ease the new philosophical trend challenged what was held very sacrosanct in social life of India. So social issues like the stratification of the society, the distinction between the pure and the polluted, the injustice meted out to common people in the name of God were questioned by this new genre of philosophers. One may describe the entire movement as the "dissident stream of spirituality". This was but a natural fallout of an approach that was responsive to social realities and the predicament of the common man. Yet very much like the Classical and the orthodox philosophical systems the philosophers of this phase discussed about the nature of the Reality, the relation between the world and the Reality, cosmogony and the path to self-realization. So it would be too brusque on our part to say that there is no philosophical mettle in such a new way of doing philosophy.

Another aspect of such non-conformism was the new way of handling the prevalent religious practices. In most cases, the thinkers of the post-Classical era delineated God as formless, Absolute, One and of indescribable presence. So idolatry along with the other frills of religious practices including meaningless rituals like elaborate *pūjās*, and fastings, were challenged. It is surprising that the most illiterate and downtrodden sections of the society accepted this new way of looking at God and religion with an open arm. The genre of thought proved how the highly speculative and abstract idea of a Supreme Being that was eulogized by Upaniṣads and Advaitism could be translated into practice. In the process these thinkers pointed out the weak links of a tradition that failed to clearly elucidate the relation between the human beings, their life and the Reality. This unique dimension of the post-Classical period needs to be discussed in detail. So, I shall devote a separate chapter to that. Besides, without keeping it in the background we would not be in a position to do proper justice to the philosophy of Mahimā Dharma.

II. Mahimā Dharma: An Overview

What inspired me to embark upon a systematic analysis of the philosophical position of Mahimā Dharma is, practically speaking, twofold. First and foremost, Mahimā Dharma is said to be the last and latest movement of post-Classical phase as it came to the fore during 1860s. Of course, during this phase India had witnessed the rise of neo-Hinduism like Brahmo Dharma, Ārya Samāj movement and many more. But they were more or less elitist movements. And most importantly, they were revivalist movements with certain nostalgia for our ancient interpretation of philosophical thinking, especially Upaniṣads and also Vedas. But Mahimā Dharma is exclusively a movement meant for the underdog. As I have stated earlier, it, like all other post-Classical movements which the scholars prefer to call as a Bhakti movement, had a certain undercurrent of defiance in its tone and tenor. Mahimā Dharma[5] is centred on the idea of God as *śūnya*. In this case God does not stand for a symbol or idol but a formless principle. Interestingly, the idea of delineating God as *śūnya* is not new to the Indian religio-philosophical tradition. We come across such appellations in Vīraśaivism, Kashmir Śaivism, the Vaiṣṇavism of Odisha, Tantric Buddhism, Dharma cult of Bengal and Nātha Dharma. But there is a fundamental distinction between all these forms of religio-philosophical systems and Mahimā interpretation of God as *śūnya*. In case of the other systems mentioned above, though God is designated as *śūnya* it is ultimately affiliated either to Śiva, Viṣṇu, Jagannātha or to Buddha. So despite marking out God as formless *śūnya* somehow or other the traditional conception of God crept in. (I shall take up for discussion the esssentials of these systems in Chap. 2.) But Mahimā Dharma makes no such compromise. As I have stated earlier the idea itself seems quite outlandish yet the thought is a part of the living faith that has not yet been relegated to the pages of history. There are several thousands of *saṁnyāsī*s and lay followers of this *dharma* not only in Odisha but also in the neighbouring states – Bengal, Chhattisgarh and Andhra.

---

5 Though the term *dharma* is prefixed to Mahimā philosophy it does not necessarily mean that it is a purely religious order without any philosophical basis. The term has been in use long since. So I use the word Mahimā Dharma.

Second, during the last two decades there has been a sudden spurt in attention to Mahimā Dharma, especially from the Western scholars. There are a large number of papers and books published on this system of thought. But the focus of such works seems to be more on the historical, sociological, anthropological, hagiographical and literary aspects of Mahimā Dharma without sufficient attention being paid on its philosophical moorings. But it remains a fact that without comprehending its philosophical structure the researchers are likely to stray into findings that sometimes might prove to be counter-effective. This is the reason why I undertook the task of unraveling the philosophical analysis of Mahimā Dharma.

Unlike the other neo-philosophical movements that continuously kept on pouring in different parts of India from thirteenth century CE onwards, Mahimā Dharma rose like a phoenix around 1860s. Its impact was so sudden and great that the British administration was forced to instruct the Commissioner of Orissa Division to submit a short report on the movement.[6] This report forms the basis for further short references in the *District Gazetteer of Sambalpur*. Despite the alleged reputation of being non-orthodox and non-Hindu movement it attracted the attention of some scholars. Around 1911 some attempts were made by two eminent scholars of Bengal to project Mahimā Dharma not just as a social movement but a movement with an embedded philosophy of its own. The first was B.C. Majumdar's work *Sonepur in the Samblapur Tract*[7] and the second was N.N. Vasu's *Modern Buddhism and Its Followers in Orissa*[8] and *The Archaeological Survey of Mayurbhanj*.[9] In these works Vasu attempted to relate Mahimā Dharma with the tribal religions on the

---

[6] There was an attack on Śrī Jagannātha Temple at Purī allegedly by a handful of Mahimā followers. The report submitted was later published in the *Proceedings of the Asiatic Society*, Bengal, 1882, pp. 2-3. The report describes Mahimā-Panthīs as a sect of Hindu dissenters.

[7] Calcutta, 1911, IV, pp. 126-36.

[8] Calcutta, 1911.

[9] Vol. I, 1911, pp. CLXLV-CCIXIII.

one hand, and with the medieval Utkalīya Vaiṣṇavism of the five *sants* of sixteenth-century Odisha, popularly known as Pañcasakhā, on the other. On the basis of the presence of certain Buddhistic elements in their philosophy he portrayed Mahimā Dharma as "neo-Buddhism". These works caught widespread attention. As a result the name of Mahimā Dharma passed into the standard works like Eliot's *Hinduism and Buddhism.*[10]

The first detailed account of Mahimā Dharma appeared almost forty years later in a long article entitled "Studies in Medieval Religion and Literature in Orissa" by Cittaranjan Das in 1950.[11] This was followed by a full-fledged work in Odiya entitled *Odisara Mahimā Dharma* in 1952. But for quite some time Odia scholars did not pay much attention either to Bhīmā Bhoi or to Mahimā Dharma till Anncharlot Eschmann's publication of a series of research papers in 1975, as a member of the First Orissa Research Project of German Scholars. Her research paper entitled "Mahimā Dharma: An Autochthonous Hindu Reform Movement"[12] covered the whole ambit of Mahimā Dharma including its philosophical presuppositions (though in a synoptic manner) in general. The Odia community should be grateful to her for undertaking all the pains to study the different dimensions of Mahimā Dharma. Subsequently a series of works and research papers have been published that include the books by Sitakanta Mohapatra, S. Nath, Bhagirathi Nepak, Siddhartha Das, Ishita Banerjee-Dube and others. All these studies chiefly highlighted on the literary, historical, institutional, sociological and anthropological aspects of the movement. The second Orissa Research Project undertaken by the German scholars in the 1990s resulted in a spate of research papers by Johannes Beltz and Lydia Guzy and also Ishita Banerjee-Dube.

---

[10] Charles Eliot, 1921, *Hinduism and Buddhism: A Historical Sketch*, vol. II, London, pp. 115f.

[11] *Visva-Bharati Annals*, vol. III, 1950, pp. 94-107.

[12] Published in H. Kulke and G.C. Tripathi (eds.), 2005, *The Cult of Jagannath and the Regional Tradition of Orissa*, New Delhi: Manohar, pp. 375-410.

But some of the research papers published especially by Johannes Beltz[13] that dealt with the personality of Bhīmā Bhoi created heavy consternation among the literati and followers of Mahimā Dharma in Odisha. The need of the hour is not writing the hagiography of the pioneers of this *dharma* but to understand its true spirit that has always stood for a new way of looking at life, world and God. It is an irony that scholars and historians love to place the philosophical essence of Mahimā Dharma under one or the other mould of the existing systems of philosophy, thereby denying its uniqueness and originality. If scholars like N.N Vasu and others present Mahimā Dharma as a form of neo-Buddhism, then as a mark of retaliation the great Avadhūta of Mahimā order, Biśvanātha Bābā makes enormous effort to prove that this system of thought is but a part of the philosophy of the Classical age and even a part of Sanātana Dharma. Biśvanātha Bābā, a great scholar of the Classical tradition, has produced voluminous works profusely quoting Śāstras and Sūtras of the Classical age, and even *Manu Saṁhitā* to prove its orthodox credentials. In the process its spirit of dissidence against the existing orthodoxy and the resultant social ramifications are totally obliterated.[14] It is almost forgotten that this *dharma* was the product of the soil that raised its head under tremendous social pressure.

As I have stated earlier there are very few scholarly works devoted entirely to the philosophical exploration of the philosophy of Mahimā Dharma. Excepting the papers by C.R.

---

[13] Johannes Beltz, 2003, "Bhīmā Bhoi: The Making of a Saint", in A. Copley (ed.), *Hinduism in Public and Private: Reform, Hindutva, Gender and Sampradaya*, New Delhi: Oxford University Press.

[14] As the Mahimā Dharma later on was divided into sects and its powerful proponents disowned Bhīmā Bhoi after the demise of the Mahimā Svāmī Biśvanātha Bābā's interpretation of Mahimā Dharma is held to be sacrosanct among a section of the Mahimā-panthīs. Despite such disclaim Bhīmā Bhoi's writings form an important part of the *bhajanas* that are sung by all the sects of the Mahimā-panthīs. I shall present my arguments over this controversial issue in Appendix.

Das[15] and B. Kar[16] and a insightful book by S.C. Panigrahi[17] we do not come across many works in English devoted solely to the philosophy of Mahimā Dharma. But something that strikes as most unusual is that all these works somehow gloss over the concept of *śūnya* that forms an important aspect of the Mahimā metaphysics. It appears that there is some eagerness on the part of the scholars to avoid the controversy that could arise from the emphasis on the word *śūnya* (though the Mahimā literature composed during the lifetime of its founder is full of the word *śūnya*). This is mostly due to the misconstrued opinion that the use of the word stands for the Buddhist affiliation despite the fact that many orthodox Indian systems of thought use the word *śūnya* to delineate the Reality Supreme. The convenient amnesia regarding the concept of *śūnya* by the scholars is a matter of regret. By shying away from undertaking an unbiased and neutral investigation of a very original philosophical position like Mahimā philosophy we are doing harm to the rich cultural tradition of India.

My explication of the philosophy of Mahimā Dharma would be solely based on the voluminous works composed by the great Kandha (a paricular tribal community) poet Bhīmā Bhoi, whom its founder Mahimā Svāmī entrusted with the task of propagating the essence of Mahimā Dharma at a very young age through his lyrical yet highly philosophical poems. Since 1865 his compositions were sung at Mahimā congregations with the full support of his master. For at least half a century his poems were considered as the only source of Mahimā ideology and became a part of the Mahimā ritual; and the practice still continues. Since Mahimā Svāmī had composed no written texts, for quite some time it left the impression among the people in general that Bhīmā Bhoi is also a kind of the founding

---

15 C.R. Das, 1950, "Studies in Medieval Religion and Literature of Orissa", *Vishva-Bharati Annals*, III: 94-107.

16 B. Kar, 1969, "Religious Philosophy of Mahimā Goswami and His School", *Bharati, Journal of Humanities*, Utkal University, 3(4).

17 S.C. Panigrahi, 1989, *Bhīmā Bhoi and Mahimā Darsana*, Bhubaneswar: D.S.A. in Philosophy, Utkal University.

personality of Mahimā Dharma. C.R. Das rightly observes that

> though Mahimā Gosain was the founder of Mahimā Dharma it was really the works of Bhīmā Bhoi, the blind poet, that brought home to all people the essence and excellence of the new doctrine. He shines with such prominence in the history of this particular religious movement that even more than one critic have taken him to be the actual founder of it.[18]

In the early phase of its development he played a crucial role in putting forth the true philosophical position of the system as much as his Master. Though in the later phase of its development, in the early part of the twentieth century, the maistream Mahimā Dharma situated at Joranda disowned Bhīmā Bhoi's importance. Despite this sad development Bhīmā Bhoi's poems are not dismissed and they are recited regularly in Mahimā congregations. Nobody can deny that in the early phases of its unprecedented popularity it was the poems of Bhīmā Bhoi that attracted people to this new form of religious practice. Since 1865 his compositions were sung at Mahimā congregations with the full support of his Master. For at least half a century his poems were considered as the only source of Mahimā ideology and the recitation and singing of the poems in the form of *bhajana*s became a part of the Mahimā ritual; and the practice still continues.

It may be noted that only in Bhīmā Bhoi's texts does one come across the basic idea of God as *śūnya*. This idea is not only reflected in his most popular works *Stuti Cintāmaṇi* and more than 200 *bhajana*s but also in such highly philosophical works like *Brahma-Nirūpaṇa Gītā*, *Śrutiniṣedha Gītā*, *Nirveda Sādhanā* and *Aṣṭakabihārī Gītā*. One gets a clear idea about his philosophical concepts like, *śūnya-Brahman*, *piṇḍa–brahmāṇḍa* identity (world as macrocosm and individual body as microcosm), *jīva–parama* identity (the identity between the individual self and the cosmic self), *niṣkāma-bhakti* and his rebellious views about eradication of social stratification (*jāti/*

[18] C.R. Das, 1982, *A Glimpse into Oriya Literature*, Bhubaneswar: Orissa Sahitya Akademi, p. 230.

varṇa-vyavasthā), idolatry and meaningless religious rites from the vast collection of his compositions. My chief task is to draw out the essence of Mahimā Dharma from his compositions. I should make it clear that my approach to the philosophical analysis of Mahimā Dharma is a rational interpretation of the system. Its philosophy is not primarily esoteric in nature, as perceived by some Western scholars. We must keep in mind that Bhīmā Bhoi, the poet-philosopher who was entrusted with the duty of spreading the message of the *dharma,* could not have made any impact on general mass had it been esoteric. As it would be gradually unfolded during the course of our discussion, most of his verses are simple and lucid to the core.

Despite the popularity of Bhīmā Bhoi's compositions, a scholar may find it difficult to get a well-organized picture of the philosophy of Mahimā Dharma as the philosophical doctrines are not presented in a very systematic manner as is observed in case of the scholastic philosophical systems from the Classical age. Yet it should not deter anybody interested in understanding the basics of Mahimā philosophy from undertaking the job. The task may be difficult, for one has to scan through his voluminous works and weave them carefully. But the challenge is rewarding.

Part I

2

God as Śūnya: Other Traditions

God as *śūnya* may appear quite a perplexing idea since scholars prefer to translate the term *śūnya* either as void or as emptiness. Both these words have negative connotation implying "nothingness". Therefore, many of us might question the authenticity of the orthopraxis of this idea. Yet it is an amazing fact that Mahimā Dharma is not the only strand of religio-philosophy which is centred on the idea of God as *śūnya.* There are handful systems of thought that subscribed to the idea. A scanning of the theories of the Indian religio-philosophical tradition reveals that Kashmir Śaivism, Vīraśaivism of Karnataka, Nātha Dharma, Tantric Buddhism, Dharma cult of Bengal and the indigenous medieval Vaiṣṇavism of Odisha belonged to this category. Though flourishing in different corners of India they shared the same view regarding the nature of God. In this chapter I would like to offer an overview of these religio-philosophical positions with special emphasis on Odia Vaiṣṇavism so that we can assess the novelty of the Mahimā philosophy. But before I proceed with the main thrust of the chapter I would like to offer a very brief idea on the genesis of the term *śūnya* and the exact implication of the term.

The Genesis of the Concept of Śūnya

Though the word *śūnya* is not unknown to the Brāhmanical tradition it was the Mādhyamika branch of Mahāyāna Buddhism that developed its metaphysics around the concept of *śūnyatā*. Nāgārjuna, who systematically pioneered Śūnyavāda, conceived *śūnyatā* as the transcendental principle (*tattva*) that eludes the conceptual forms and categories of human thinking. This all-comprehensive principle is the highest *tattva* that according to

Nāgārjuna "can be directly realized, which is calm and blissful, that where all plurality is merged, that where all cries of intellect are satisfied. In other words it is the non-dual harmonious whole."[1] As our concept formation requires determination and discrimination, and any attempt to determine a concept through predication of a quality implies negation of its opposite, it is best described as inconceivable. Any attempt to apply a predicate to such a principle leads to limitation as well as discrimination and duality, whereas the Reality is non-dual (*advaya*). Thus the ultimate reality is *catuṣkoṭi vinirmukta*, i.e. it is beyond the fourfold forms of categorization.[2] In other words, *śūnyatā* signifies a principle about which neither existence nor non-existence, nor a combination of both nor the negation of both, can be predicated. Such a reality is *niḥsvabhāva* (without essence) and *niṣprapañca* (without categories). Nāgārjuna's conception of *śūnyatā* corresponds to the *tathatā* of Aśvaghoṣa, the founder of Mahāyāna Buddhism, who said that reality cannot be comprehended by concepts but can only be experienced as pure *suchness*. Thus *śūnya* is not a negative expression but connotes ineffability. That is to say, *śūnya* is not a mere naught but simply the absence of characteristics. Human language is the manifestation of thought and thought is limited and conditioned. Our verbalization, speech and thought are determined by concepts. Thus describing the reality as *śūnyatā* is a makeshift way of verbalizing a principle that is beyond verbalization. Yet despite such limitations speech is the only instrument human beings have at their disposal. That is why the Buddha had always insisted on the middle path in order to avoid both extremes – (1) negating too pervasively, and (2) not negating sufficiently. The first leads to Ucchedavāda (nihilism) and

---

[1] *aparam pratyayaṁśānaṁ prapañciraprapañcitam* ।
nirvikalpam anayarthamr̥tat tattvasya lakṣaṇam ॥
– *Mādhyamika-Kārikā* XVIII.9

[2] *atastattvam sadsad ubhayānubhayātmaka catuṣkoṭi vinirmuktam śūnya meva*.

Sarvadarśana Saṁgraha of Madhvācārya tr. with Sanskrit texts by E.B. Cowell and A.E. Gough, ed. K.L. Joshi, Delhi: Parimal Publications, 1980, p. 30.

the second leads to Śāśvatavāda (eternalism). Staying away from both these extremes and understanding suchness between them is the "middle path" or Mādhyamika. So *śūnya* is not emptiness or void. As Antony Kalliath rightly observes:

> "No-thing" means "there-is-no-thing"; where there is "no-thing", there is immense room for everything.[3]

Śūnya is the womb of inexhaustible creative potential and a vortex of movement and energy. Thus the word *śūnyatā* in the Buddhist context does not mean either "void" or "emptiness", though most of the scholars prefer to translate the word so. Perhaps the word *śūnyatā* has no English. This is the reason why I have preferred to keep the term *śūnya* intact. This word like the word *Brahman* should not be diluted through translation.

We can be in a better position to grasp the real implication of the word *śūnya* if we have a look at its etymological root. *Śūnya* is derived from the root *svi* implying "to swell". The ancient Indian mathematicians used the term *śūnya* as a number signifying the infinite (*ananta*) thereby turning it into the matrix of all the numbers. Explicating the significance of *śūnya* as the number zero further, Varāhamihira, the great ancient mathematician, stated that what makes all numbers swell is *śūnya*. There is no change in the infinite, thereby implying that there is no change in *śūnya* either by addition or subtraction. This mathematical implication of the term *śūnya* provides very valuable clue to one's understanding of the Mādhyamika notion of *śūnyatā*.

The idea of *śūnya*, though not entirely unknown to the Upaniṣadic and Vedic culture, is also not a very popular concept in the Brāhmanical tradition either. Texts like *Śrī-Bhāgavatam* and *Mahopaniṣad* describe *parama Brahman* as *śūnyavat*. Of course, in such texts the word *śūnyavat* does not signify pure negation. In *Śrīmad*

---

[3] A. Kalliatha, 2005, "Pūrṇam-Śūnya-Pleroma as Communion of Beings", in Bettina Bäumer and J.R. Dupuche (eds.) *Void and Fullness in the Buddhist, Hindu and Christian Traditions: Śūnya-Pūrṇa-Plerôma*, New Delhi: D.K. Printworld, p. 220.

Bhāgavatam whenever the word *śūnya* is used, it signifies a state of indescribability. Let us examine the following verse from this work that uses the word *śūnya* to explicate the state of *suṣupti.*

saṁsuptavat śūnyavat apatakyaṁ ।
tatmūlabhūtaṁ padamamananti ॥ – 12.4.21

The *ṭīkākāra* of the work clarifies that *śūnyavat* stands for *śūnyamivasthitaṁ na tu śūnyamityarthaḥ* (it resides in *śūnya,* it does not mean *śūnya*).[4] Similarly, Śaṅkarācārya, in his commentary on *Viṣṇu Sahasranāma* explicates the meaning of the word *śūnyavat* as *saviśeṣarahita tvāt śūnyavat* (it is without determination, hence like *śūnya*). Thus even in the orthodox tradition *śūnya* does not have a negative meaning. But at the same time it must be admitted that the use of the word *śūnya* in orthodox tradition is quite sporadic. None of the orthodox (*āstika*) schools of Indian philosophy prefers to use the epithet *śūnya* in the context of the Highest Reality. This explains why Śaṅkarācārya preferred to refute Śūnyavāda as a form of Ucchedavāda.

Following the clue provided by the ancient mathematicians we can as well say *śūnyatā* – the non-dual harmonious whole – is but another name for *pūrṇa* – the all-comprehensive principle that remains unchanged through addition and subtraction. This reminds us of the famous Upaniṣadic *mantra* that delineates *Brahman* as *pūrṇa.*[5] The concept of *pūrṇa* defies any scope for addition, subtraction, multiplication or division. So, as far as the etymological and connotative significance is concerned, the conceptual contour of the terms *śūnya, Brahman* and *pūrṇa* is almost the same. Unfortunately, it is the philosophers who create a conceptual gap. The Buddhists were averse to the word *Brahman* and similarly the word *śūnya* did not find much favour in orthodox Brāhmanical literature.

---

[4] References cited form N. Pradhan, 1986, *Prācīna Odia Sāhityare Nirguṇa Dhārā,* Cuttack: Dharma Grantha Store, p. 98.

[5] *oṁ pūrṇmadaḥ pūrṇamidam pūrṇāt pūrṇamudacyate* ।
pūrṇasya pūrṇamādāya pūrṇamevāvaśiṣyate ॥ – Mantra of *Īśopaniṣad*

The Spirit of Assimilation

Before I proceed on with the task I would expect the scholars and academicians to overcome a powerful dogma that is likely to stand in our way of understanding the true kernel of the *śūnya*-centric metaphysics. At academic level there is a tendency to draw a clear-cut conceptual boundary that clinically separates one system of thought from another. As academic scholars have ignored the philosophical development in India in the post-Rāmānuja phase they seldom realize the fact that the nature of philosophical enterprise underwent radical change in the post-Classical phase. The period is a marked by a perceptible effort to translate philosophy into action. The shift was from speculation to practice. So the watertight distinction between the *āstika* and *nāstika* traditions coalesced. There was an imperceptible interpenetration between the two streams. Therefore the demarcating lines between the two had become indefinite and their differences less fundamental. The concept of *ātman* and also of *yoga* as a method of *sādhanā*, that was taken as the trademark of *āstika* system, was incorporated in the Buddhist and Jaina traditions. The literature of Vajrayāna Buddhists can be cited as a case in point.[6] Similarly, the critical approach of the *nāstika* school had penetrated into the Brāhmanical tradition also. The texts like *Yogavāsiṣṭha Rāmāyaṇa* can be taken as the finest example of such a spirit of accommodation. We notice that this syncretic trend in the philosophical systems that subscribes to the theory of God as *śūnya* also simultaneously adheres to non-dualism (Advaita), which is often regarded as typically a Brāhmanical concept.

---

[6] Vajrayāna admits the role of *yoga* in self-realization. They call it *svadhidaivata yoga*. Similarly, Vajrayāna in certain cases talk of *ātman*.

bodhicittam idaṁ vajraṁ sarvabuddhatvam ātmanaḥ ।
tasmāt sarvātma-yogena sarvabuddhatvam āpnute ॥ – *Jñāna Siddhi*, XV

Quoted in B. Dasgupta, 1974, *Introduction to Tantric Buddhism*, Calcutta: University of Calcutta, 1974, p. 83.

God as Śūnya in Śaivism

KASHMIR ŚAIVISM

One comes across the concept of *śūnya* used in a very significant sense, at least, in some of the sects of Śaivism. Of these one flourished in the extreme north and is known as Kashmir Śaivism. This form of Śaivism, otherwise known as Śivādvaitism, evolved sometime in the eighth-ninth century CE and continued with its glory till twelfth century CE. Kashmir Śaivism is associated with great names as Somānanda and Abhinavagupta. But Śivādvaitism, despite its designating the Reality Supreme as ineffable, non-conceptualizable, non-dual principle (Advaita), should not be confused with the Advaitism of Śaṅkara. In this case the phenomenal world is not understood as the product of the *māyā* or a case superimposition, as we notice in the case of Advaitism. According to Kashmir Śaivism the universe is the real manifestation of God. Rather they prefer the word "emanation". For them, *sṛṣṭi* implies "emanation", not "creation"; similarly, the word *saṁhāra* means "re-absorption" rather than "destruction". Hence the Primal Reality or Parama-Śiva is the potential ground of the universe. It is the source from which everything emerges and into which everything merges.

Kashmir Śaivism subscribes to a form of strict non-dualism (Advaita). According to this system the Reality Supreme is a principle beyond description, beyond manifestation, beyond the limits of form, time and space. This is all-pervading, all-knowing and ineffable in nature. Though the theory comes closest to the Upaniṣadic *Brahman* yet the theory dismisses the Vedic connection and is more dependent on the tantric theories for its interpretation of the Ultimate Reality. Unlike Upaniṣads and Śaṅkara's Advaitism, Kashmir Śaivism talks of *śakti* (implying the force or energy) as an integral part of Parama-Śiva. The Ultimate Reality is also depicted as of the nature of *śūnya* as is obvious from a verse of *Vijñāna-Bhairava*, one of the most practice-oriented texts of Kashmir Śaivism:

> . . . the unknowable, the ungraspable, the void (*śūnya*), that which pervades non-existence, contemplate on all this as Bhairava. At

> the end (of this contemplation) illumination will dawn.[7]

A close look at the text reveals that the concept of *śūnya* plays a unique role in this philosophy. Interestingly, though Advaitic in spirit and despite addressing the Supreme Reality as one and ineffable, it subscribes to the theory of *bhakti*. But here *bhakti* does not signify emotional attachment to the God but an intricate process of meditation (*yoga*). This helps them to use the concept of *śūnya* with diverse dimensions and sometimes with diverse significance. This is evident from the fact that this text talks of three dimensions of *śūnya*, one leading to the other. At the level of the human beings *śūnya* is the condition. The practitioner has to realize that *saṁsāra* is *śūnya*. He has to detach himself from the world. Again he achieves his goal through the supreme energy of *śūnya*. So *śūnya* is the means. Finally the Ultimate Reality is *śūnyatā* itself.[8] This supreme *śūnya* is also known as *anuttatra* (unsurpassable) *śūnya* and *advaya śūnya*. Thus not only are end and means of self-realization *śūnya* but also by the experience of the power of *śūnya* the seeker becomes *śūnya* and assumes the form of *śūnya* itself (*śūnyākāra*).

> *śūnyāya śūnyto 'sau śūnyākāraḥ pumān bhavet* । – V.40

In this case the *bhakta* who is also a meditator finally realizes the void nature of everything.

> . . . If one imagines this whole universe as *śūnya*, one's mind gets dissolved in it and becomes worthy of merging in that (supreme *śūnya*).[9]

---

[7] Quoted from Bettina Bäumer, 2005, "Attaining the Form of the Void: Śūnya in the Vijñana-Bhairava", in *Void and Fullness in Hindu, Buddhist and Christian Traditions*, ed. Bettina Bäumer and J.R. Dupuche, New Delhi: D.K. Printworld, p. 169.

[8] *śūnyāya paraya śaktya śūnyatam eti bhairavī* । – V 39. Quoted in Bäumer 2005: 169

[9] *viśvam-etān mahādevī śūnya-bhūtam vicintayet* ।
tatraiva ca monolīnaḥ tatas-tallaya-bhājanam ॥
– Quoted in Bäumer 2005: 168

According to some scholars[10] the word *śūnya* is incorporated into Kashmir Śaivism from Mahāyāna Buddhism that had a strong presence in the area. This is a matter that should be probed further. But Śivādvaitism would not like to affiliate itself to any form of Buddhism. It is a part of the *āstika* tradition though it decried Veda and opposed the interpretation of the word *śūnya* as nothing-ness. So they make it clear that *śūnya* is not *abhāva* (absence) but *sadbhāva* implying thereby a state of total mergence of everything and being. This is obvious from the following *śloka*:

> *aśūnyam śūnyam it uktam, śūnyāt abhāva ucyate* ।
> *abhāvastu vijñyeyo yatrabhāva layam gata* ॥[11]

> *Śūnya* is *aśūnya*, not the condition of the emptiness. *Śūnya* is said to be *abhāva* because it refers to a state in which objects (*bhāva*) lie in the total mergence. In Śiva's consciousness supreme, the entire creation is in a state of total mergence – without name and form – a state of dilution. It is indistinguishable from the Śiva's supreme consciousness.

From the above *śloka* it becomes obvious that the word *śūnya* indicates the sense, *pūrṇa*. I have discussed earlier about this implicit connotation of the term. But Kashmir Śaivism seems to offer an interesting interpretation of the term. According to it the Highest Reality also could be conceived as a positive being (*sattāmātra*). So the highest *śūnya* is described as utmost fullness (*atyanta pūrṇatā*). It contains everything in itself and materializes everything in the concrete form of this physical and subtle universe. *Svacchanda Tantra*, another seminal text of the Āgama literature of Kashmir Śaivism, says:

> *tatra tatra param śūnyaṁ sarvaṁ vyāpya vyvasthitam* ।
> *tadeva bhavati sthūlam sthūlopādhivasāt priye* ॥[12]

---

10 M.L. Kaul, "The Concept Śūnya from Buddhism to Kasmir Śaivism to Lalla Ded", ikashmir.net/milout sunya.html.

11 Quoted in Kaul.

12 Quoted from M.L. Kokiloo, 2005, "Concept of Fullness: Pūrṇatā in Kashmir Śaivism", in *Void and Fullness in Hindu, Buddhist and Christian Traditions*, New Delhi: D.K. Printworld, p. 117.

The tradition was further cultivated by Lal Dêd. She wrote in the form of verse (*bakh*) in the regional language. She conceives Parama Śiva as *anāhata, kha svarūpa* and *śūnya lai. Kha* is a word often used in Buddhist literature to signify *śūnya*. As I have pointed out earlier, the dogma about composing treatises in Sanskrit as the benchmark of attaining the status of *darśana* could be noticed in Lal Dêd too. Since the texts of Kashmir Śaivism are composed in Sanskrit it is known as *darśana* (often called as Trika *darśana*). As Lal Dêd was responsible for spreading the philosophy of Śivādvaitism among the common man in regional language, she has not attracted the attention of the posterity. She is regarded as a *sant*, not a philosopher.

VĪRAŚAIVISM

Another form of Śaivism that attained popularity in the southern part of India is almost as old as Kashmir Śaivism. The central figure of Śaiva Siddhānta is Allama Prabhu who took a leading part in the reformatory movement led by Basaveśvara. This form of Śaivism is also uncompromisingly non-dualist in its stance. *Śūnya Sampādana,* the compilation of the discourses of Allama Prabhu in the *vacana* form, is presumed to be composed sometime in fifteenth century. According to him the Ultimate Reality is *śūnya* Śiva. He is beyond comprehension and description. It is beyond all the categories of thought – positive as well as negative. Thus it is addressed as *śūnya*. The Absolute Reality is described as the only one (*ekam*), eternal (*nitya*) and beyond contradictions (*dvandvātītam*). It is perfect and complete in every respect. This description makes it clear that the description of the Para-Śiva is not negative. Here *śūnya* is used in the sense of *pūrṇa*. The Highest Reality as per the metaphysics of Vīraśaivism, though close to the Upaniṣadic ideal of *Brahman* is not an abstract principle but a Being who can be meditated upon and worshipped. So the text emphasizes the notion of *śaraṇa*, i.e. taking refuge. One who has taken refuge aims to attain (*sampādana*) this supreme state (*śūnya*). Naturally, the text is practice-oriented and talks of several steps for the attainment of the highest state.

Much like Kashmir Śaivism, Vīraśaivism too subscribes to

the view that the phenomenal world is an emanation from God. The process of emanation starts as soon as Para-Śiva becomes conscious of His being in the form of "I am". In a sense Para-Śiva is the potential ground of the varied and variegated forms of the phenomenal world. It is indivisible, without a second (*advaya*), existence-consciousness-bliss (*saccidānanda*), eternal and beyond all contradictions of positive and negative predicates. At this stage Śiva is *śūnya*. Allama Prabhu describes this state of the Highest Reality in the following way:

O Lord, this is the true height of the form
Of the undivided Absolute Divine.
It is neither form nor formlessness,
This undivided form of the Absolute
It is neither of this (time) nor of timelessness;
It is neither of this (world) nor of the other world,
Not touched by sorrow or by joy,
Above all merit and sin.
It is neither cause nor consequence,
Not bound by duty or works,
Nor worshipped nor worshipper.
Thus being beyond the sense of twain
He shines – our Guhyeśvaraliṅga.[13]

These lines bring out to the surface the description of a Being who can only be approached either by negative predication or contradictory predication. Naturally such a being is beyond description and human conception. And that is what is meant by *śūnya* as well as *pūrṇa*. So according to Vīraśaivism, Para-Śiva (the Highest Reality) in its primal form is complete void (*sarva-śūnya*) and without support. He exists as the power that can at best be described by *oṁkāra nirañjana śakti*. He is also designated as *Niṣkala-Brahman* (the undifferentiated *Brahman*). This power manifests itself as the world in the following order. The *sarva-śūnya* is manifested as *śūnyaliṅga* which is further manifested as

[13] Quoted from Rama Ghose, "Śūnya Sampādana: A Mystical Concept of Vīraśaivism", in Bettina Bäumer (ed.) *Void and Fullness*, p. 203.

mahāliṅga. From *mahāliṅga* emerges Sadāśiva with five faces that are related to five elements of the phenomenal world, viz. earth, water, air, light and ether. Thus the whole universe is permeated by the power of the highest Being – the Para-Śiva.

NĀTHA DHARMA

Nātha cult may be included within the fold of Śaivism, but it cannot be said to be a pure and orthodox *āstika* system of thought. I have already mentioned that during the post-Classical period there was a happy amalgamation of the so-called dichotomy between *āstika* and *nāstika* philosophical traditions. If we go by the definition of *āstika* vs. *nāstika* division then a *āstika* system is that which owes its allegiance to Veda and Vedic injunctions (whether practically it is followed or not). But so far as the systems of philosophy I have discussed in this chapter are concerned, none of them owes its allegiance to the Vedic injunctions. For example, Kashmir Śaivism draws its support from Tantra. On the other hand, Vīraśaivism was considered if not as a protestant movement, at least a reformatory movement. Similarly, Nātha Dharma, though puritanical in nature, cannot be said to be a direct offshoot of the so-called *āstika* line of thinking.

Nātha Dharma that rose into prominence during ninth century also depicts the highest Reality as *śūnya* as well as *nirguṇa*. The history and legends of this *dharma* recognize Gorakhanātha as the founder of this religion. Sometimes, Mīnanātha or Matsyendranātha, his preceptor, is also taken to be one of the earliest *yogī*s of this *dharma*. Interestingly both of them figure prominently in the list of eighty-four *siddha*s of Tantric Buddhism too. This indicates that there must have been some close link between Nātha Dharma and Tantric Buddhism. It is possible that Gorakhanātha and Matsyendranātha broke away from Tantric Buddhism due to the preponderance of sexo-yogic practices encouraged by the former. So Nāthism is more puritanical and ethico-centric in nature. As far as the metaphysics of this *dharma* is concerned, one clearly notes the shadow of Mahāyānic as well as Advaitic interpretation of the Reality. The Reality is projected as *nirañjana* (taintless), *śūnya*, *nirguṇa* (non-qualifiable) and *anādi* (beginningless). Positively, they describe the principle as *Para-Brahman*. As the all-pervading, self-existing, eternal and Absolute Reality, it is also depicted as pure consciousness, pure existence and pure bliss (*sat–cit–ānanda*). But such a Reality is not an abstract principle like the Upaniṣadic *Brahman* but an object of devotion. This Reality Supreme is also identified as Ādinātha or Śiva.[14] But from this we cannot jump into the conclusion that Nātha Dharma is purely a product of *āstika* tradition. Rather we come across a wonderful syncretism of the *āstika* and *nāstika* traditions. A little probe shows that as far as the non-dualistic metaphysics of the Nātha Dharma is concerned there is not much of conceptual gap between the Nātha conception of Ādinātha and the Vajrayānic conception of Vajrasattva. Both are conceived as the ineffable one and unique reality, yet these two concepts signify a Reality that can be an object of meditation, prayer and devotion. Here Nātha Dharma deviates from the major trend, Upaniṣadic Advaitism. So the use of the word *Brahman* does not make its philosophical position purely orthodox and Brāhmanical in nature. Nor can it be called a part of the *bhakti* theory in the narrowest sense of the term. Its entire theory hinges on the theory of *yoga*, famously known as *haṭha-yoga*.

Very much like the other systems of Śaivism discussed above Nātha Dharma relies on the theory that the final realization is a super sensuous, super mental state in which the empirical consciousness is transformed into unconditioned purified perfect consciousness; and the Ultimate Reality is directly experienced not only as the object of experience but also as the experience itself. So Nātha philosophers delineate the highest state of self-realization in the following way: "It is the state in which an enlightened *yogī* fails to identify the Reality as *sat* or *asat*, *śūnya* or *pūrṇa*, *dvaita* or *advaita*, because it is beyond all categories".[15] They therefore designate their philosophical position as Dvaitādvaita-Vilakṣaṇa-Vāda. Thus like all other forms of non-dualism discussed in this chapter, Nātha

---

[14] K. Bannerjee, 1961, *The Philosophy of Gorakhanath*, Gorakhpur, Mahanta Digvijayanatha Trust, p. 47.

[15] Bannerjee 1961: 54ff.

Dharma believes in the unity of the individual soul and cosmic soul through *yoga*. Though the idea of *yoga* as a path of self-realization as well as the identity between *ātman* and *paramātman* are not quite new to the Indian philosophical tradition, Nātha Dharma treads a new path by identifying the human body (*piṇḍa*) as with the cosmic body (*brahmāṇḍa*). The universe is seen as the macrocosm and the individual body (*piṇḍa*) is the microcosm. *Siddha-Siddhānta-Paddhati*, a major text of the Nātha Dharma states, "Whatever is in the *brahmāṇḍa* is in the *piṇḍa* too".[16] Thereby the theory highlights the presence of the divinity within the body. The idea might appear quite queer in the philosophical and social context of that period. Though our body was considered as *annamaya Brahman* in Upaniṣads, in the later phases body was looked at as profane. So a lot of emphasis was laid on purifying the body through ritual bathing and the torture of the body. But the idea is almost reversed here. The theory of *kāya-sādhanā* is the direct fall out of the *piṇḍa–brahmāṇḍa tattva*. As a corollary to the control of mind through *yoga*, Nātha Dharma holds that the body should be fit enough to be a seat of the divinity. Therefore emphasis is laid on the culture of the body. This is known as *kāya-sādhanā*. As far as the theory of *piṇḍa–brahmāṇḍa* identity and the theories of *kāya-sādhanā* are concerned one may decipher an uncanny affinity with the theory of Buddhist Sahajayāna. Lakṣmīṅkara, the famous woman *siddha* of the Sahajayāna order of the Tantric Buddhism, has declared:

> No suffering, no fasting, no bathing, no purification, nor other rules of society are necessary, nor do you need to bow down before the images of gods, which are constructed out of wood, stone or mud; but you should with concentration offer worship to your body where all gods reside.[17]

---

[16] *brahmāṇḍavarti yat kiñcit tat piṇḍe haryaste sarvathā* ।
– *Siddha-Siddhānta-Paddhati*, 3.2. quoted in N. Pradhan, 1986, *Prācīna Oriyā Sāhityare Nirguṇara Dhārā*, Cuttack: Dharma Grantha Store, p. 304

[17] *na kaṣṭa kalpanāṁ kuryāt nopavāso*
na ca kriyām ।
snānaṁ śaucaṁ

→

The Nātha Dharma played a huge role in shaping up of the *nirguṇa-panthī* philosophy voiced by such great *sant*s as Kabīr, Dādū, Rajjab, the Vaiṣṇavism of Odisha and also Mahimā Dharma. This *dharma* too had been hugely popular in Odisha. This is evident from such works as *Śiśu Veda, Amarakośa* and *Gorekha–Hadipa Saṁvāda*. At this point it will be of some interest to note that Nātha Dharma explicitly professes both, non-idolatry and equality of one and all. Both of these presumptions are anti-Vedic. One may find a close similarity between Nātha Dharma and Mahimā Dharma which shall be elaborated later.

God as Śūnya in Buddhism

Now we come to discuss a system of thought that can be said to be purely a *nāstika* stream of thought. But if we look deeper then we notice that during eighth to ninth CE Buddhism has undergone a lot of modifications. The tantric elements were incorporated in Buddhism, though we are not sure if tantric philosophy is orthodox or non-orthodox in origin. However, Vajrayāna as a tantric version of Mahāyāna became popular in certain parts of India, Nepal and Tibet, and continues to be a living philosophy till date. This version of Tantric Buddhism sticks to the original interpretation of *śūnyatā* as the ineffable, incomprehensible Highest Reality. But at the same time it epitomizes *śūnyatā* in the form of the Vajrasattva. Not only this, they also project Him as the ultimate object of meditation and devotion. Thus Vajrayāna, the tantric branch of Mahāyāna Buddhism, offered a religious turn to Mahāyāna Buddhism and conceived *śūnyatā* not only as the metaphysical principle but as an object of devotion too. According to them, "*śūnyatā* is said to be *vajra* (*śūnyatā vajram ityuktam*) and all manifestation in form is said to be *sattva*; so

---

← *na caivātra grāmadharma vivarjanam* ॥
na cāpi vandayeddevān kāṣṭha pāṣāṇa mṛṇmayān ।
pūjāmasyaiva kāyasya kuryānnityaṁ samāhitaḥ ॥
– B. Bhattacharyya, 1989, *An Introduction to Buddhist Esoterism*, Delhi: Motilal Banarsidass, p. 77

Vajrasattva implies the unity and identity of the two".[18] This school of Buddhism further believes that even if Vajrasattva is free from all existence and non-existence, even if He transcends all conceptual categorization, yet he is the God (*Bhagavān*); and the potential ground of the phenomenal world. *Vyakta Bhāvānugata Tattva Siddhi*, an important Vajrayāna text, therefore states that "He is the God unparalleled, revealer of potential thoughts".[19]

Vajrasattva is believed to be the perfect embodiment *śūnyatā* as well as consciousness. Indrabhūti, the great *siddha* of this order articulates the nature of this Reality in the following way:

> He is the being without origination and destruction, the all good, the soul substance of all, the enlightened one encompassing within him all that is static and dynamic. . . . He eternally belongs to all elements, to all beings – he remains pervading all bodies in the form of flow of consciousness, he is immutable, unthinkable, passionless, *śūnya* like the sky, free from existence and non-existence.[20]

We must note that Vajrayānic conception of Vajrasattva cannot be called a form of theism in the strictest sense of the term. It makes a reconciliation between the incomprehensibility of the Highest Reality with the subtle presence of God. Vajrasattva is not exactly a personal God. This is evident from the following remark in the text entitled *Anaṅgavajra Saṁgraha*:

> The deities are nothing but the manifestation of *śūnya*; and wherever there is manifestation it is *śūnya* in essence.[21]

---

[18] *śūnytāvajram ityuktam, ākāraḥ sattā ucyate* ।
tādātmyamonoyor aikyaṁ vajrasattvam iti smaraḥ ॥
– *Jvālāvalī Vajramālā Tantra;* Quoted in S.B. Dasgupta, 1974, *Introduction to Tantric Buddhism*, Calcutta: University of Calcutta, p. 78

[19] Quoted in Dasgupta 1974: 80.

[20] Ibid., p. 78.

[21] Quoted in B. Bhattacharyya, 1988, *Buddhist Esoterism*, Delhi: Motilal Banarsidass, p. 109.

S.B. Dasgupta while analysing the genesis of such an interesting theory of personal God argues that this idea has evolved from the Mahāyānic notion of *dharmakāya* of the Buddha. The early Buddhists conceived Buddha as a historical person. But Mahāyāna Buddhism transformed Buddha into the Ultimate Principle – "the totality of things or the principle of cosmic unity". The Highest Principle is believed to have three aspects known as the *trikāya*s of the Buddha, viz. *dharmakāya*, *saṁbhogakāya* and *nirmāṇakāya*. In Mahāyāna texts the word *dharma* usually signifies entity, so *dharmakāya* stands for that-ness (*tathatā rūpa*) of all entities. In other words, it is the *dharmadhātu* (primordial element) underlying all that exists. *Saṁbhogakāya*, on the other hand, signifies "the body of bliss". It manifests in the *bodhicitta*s (enlightened persons) and *nirmāṇakāya* refers to the historical personage of Buddha or the body of transformation. The concept of *dharmakāya* plays an important role in Tantric Buddhism for the evolution of the theory of Vajrasattva. Thus what is tacitly implied in Mahāyāna is fully developed by the Vajrayānīs into a non-dualistic theism.[22]

Like all other forms of the theories that conceive God as *śūnya* Vajrayāna too is only non-dualistic but subscribes to the theory of *yoga* as a method of self-realization. The goal of the seeker is to realize that there is non-difference between the transcendental Being and the individual self. Merging of the individual self with the *śuddhātman* or *paramātman* the pure existence of Buddha could be achieved through secret yogic practice. Vajrayāna, almost in Upaniṣadic light, claims that a person who realizes *himself* becomes Vajrasattva. In other words Vajrasattva-hood can be realized through conceiving all created beings as the self.[23]

This form of Buddhism had tremendous influence on Orissa, as is evident from such works of this genre in texts like *Jñānasiddhi*, (composed by Indrabhūti, the king of the Sambalaka region of

---

[22] Quoted in Dasgupta 1974: 57-58.

[23] *bodhicittam idam vajram sarva-buddhatvam ātmanaḥ* ।
— *Jñānasiddhi* XV; see *Introduction to Tantric Buddhism* in S.B. Dasgupta, p. 83

Orissa) and the Odia texts like the Buddhist Caryā literature and *Vīrasiṅgha Cautīsa*. In all probability the form of Vaiṣṇavism that was indigenous to Odisha was highly influenced by Vajrayāna Buddhism and Nātha Dharma. The conception of Jagannātha as *Śūnya-Puruṣa* bears definite stamp of these two systems of thought.

Dharma Sect of Bengal

Dharma cult (which in no way is a form of *sant* movement) is an obscure religious cult that flourished in the south-western region of Bengal. It seems that this cult remained in the oblivion for quite some time. Scholars like Mm. H.P. Sastri and N.N. Vasu brought it to limelight. Vasu published the most celebrated compendium of this order entitled *Śūnya Purāṇa* ascribed to Ramai Paṇḍit, the founder of this cult, though the original text was known as *Hakanda Purāṇa*. Scholars like S.B. Dasgupta and Suniti Kumar Chattopadhyaya are of the opinion that this text might have been composed not earlier than eighteenth century CE. Another text of this order entitled *Dharma-Pūjā-Bidhāna* is of much later origin. In his book *Modern Buddhism and Its Followers in Orissa,* Vasu claims that since Tantric Buddhism had a strong presence in certain parts of Bengal, Dharma cult is an offshoot of this form of Buddhism.

Let me now try to provide a brief outline of the basics of the Dharma cult. It owes its name to the central figure of the religion, viz. Dharma Ṭhākura. This primal deity of the cult is described as *nirañjana, nirākāra* and *śūnyadeva;* He is "beyond all positive and negative attributes. He is of the form of *śūnya* (*śūnyarūpam*) and formless saviour of all".[24] Dharma cult also indicates that the whole cosmos is nothing but evolution from the state of *śūnya*.[25] But *Śūnya Purāṇa* does not dwell much on elaborating any metaphysical position. Rather the whole text is full of instructions about certain

---

[24] *śūnyarūpam nirākāram sahsrabighnanāśanam* ı
sarva paraḥ parodevaḥ tasmāttam varobhava ıı – Atha Tika Pabana, *Śūnya Purāṇa*, ed. Bhaktimadhav Chattopadhya (Bengali), Calcutta: Firma KLM, 1977, p. 152

[25] *Śūnya Purāṇa*, Sr̥ṣṭi Pattana.

obscure religious ritualistic practices.

Dharma-Pūjā-Bidhāna, the other text of this order, seems to be more explicit as far as the concept of *śūnya* and the *śūnya*-centric theology are concerned. Special reference may be made to the passage of "Meditation on the Dharma" of this text.

> Let the Lord of the form of vacuity (*śūnya*), who has neither end, nor middle nor beginning, neither hands nor legs, neither body nor voice, neither form nor primordial self, nor fear, nor death, nor even birth – who is accessible to *yogins* in deep meditation, who permeates all sects (or who permeates all petals of the lotuses within the body) who is bereft of mental constructions, who is one, stainless, giver of the boon of immortality, protect me.[26]

The passage provides us sufficient clue about its metaphysical position. Dharma Ṭhākura is seen as an ineffable, indescribable, Absolute Reality, who could be realized only through *yoga*. Thus far it seems to have close affinity with the other schools of *śūnya*-centric metaphysics. But in both the texts there is metaphysics put forth very sporadically. The philosophical elements seem to lose its way in the maze of a very inconsistent form of religion. Sometimes Dharma Ṭhākura is identified with the God of Dharma, viz. Yama; sometimes with Viṣṇu; sometimes with Śiva; sometimes with the Sun god. As Dasgupta rightly observes, the book contains *mantras* and injunctions "regarding not only of Dharma Ṭhākura but almost all the gods and goddesses of popular Hindu Pantheon, of esoteric Buddhism as well as the pure local deities of indigenous origin".[27] As far as Vasu's claim regarding the Buddhistic origin of this cult is concerned, the entire argument seems to be based on the use of the word *śūnya* in the texts of this cult. But there is no direct reference to Buddha, as it happens with Odishan Vaiṣṇavism, wherein the Lord Supreme is addressed as Buddha-Jagannātha. What surprises us most is that whenever any reference to Buddha is made in this

---

[26] Quoted in S.B. Dasgupta, 1976, *Obscure Religious Cults*, Calcutta: Firma KLM, p. 287.

[27] Ibid., p. 405.

text it is always in the context of Jagannātha of Odisha.[28] Thus Dharma cult in the true sense of the term cannot be called a system of philosophy that rests on the idea of God as *śūnya*.

Vaiṣṇavism of Odisha (Utkalīya Vaiṣṇavism)

The metaphysical position based on the conception of *śūnya* can be said to be one of the most original contributions of the Odia *sant* philosophers in the development of history of ideas. The concept cannot be put into the straightjacket of any available philosophical mould, not even the prevalent *nirguṇa-bhakti* theory of the medieval period. Their theory of *Śūnya-Brahman/Puruṣa* is also unique in the sense that though the pioneers of this form of philosophy are self-acclaimed Vaiṣṇavas there is but very little trace of the tenets of Vaiṣṇavism in this form of philosophy. No other form of Vaiṣṇavism in India would like to conceive God as *śūnya*, no other form of Vaiṣṇavism would like to portray God as nameless, formless, attributeless, ineffable Reality. Not only this, these Odia philosophers of the post-Classical phase (fifteenth to eighteenth century CE) could, with an extraordinary ease, roll in contrasting conceptual binaries – *Śūnya* and *Brahman*, Jagannātha (who by that time was fully admitted as the Vaiṣṇavite deity) and Buddha, into one whole. This gave rise to a form of non-dualistic philosophy that defied all the metaphysical principles adhered by the traditional Brāhmanism as well Vaiṣṇavism. Like Vīraśaivism and Nātha Dharma it was a metaphysical theory aimed at enlightening the commonest of the common. As a result this atypical movement did not just remain confined to theory but was whole-heartedly accepted by the non-elite mass who had neither the time nor the inclination to understand the sophistry of Upaniṣads or Mahāyāna texts.

The idea of *śūnya* plays a pivotal role in Odishan culture and philosophy since fifteenth century CE or even much prior to that. The earliest Odia works of Nātha Dharma like *Śiśu Veda, Vedāntasāra, Śrī Gītā Sāra* and *Gorekha–Hadipa Saṁvāda* and of Tantric Buddhism like *Vīrasiṅgha Cautīsa* and *Lohi Gītā*, believed

[28] *Śūnya Purāṇa*, pp. 198-200.

to be composed between thirteenth and fourteenth century CE, frequently refer to the concept of *śūnya*. A thorough scanning of the Odia literature since thirteenth century reveals that the word *śūnya* had so much been ingrained in the Odia psyche of the period that nobody seemed to bother much about its origin. But it was Sant Sāralā Dāsa who took the first step towards the evolution of a new tradition by identifying Jagannātha with the Buddha, as well as, *śūnya*. This point of convergence takes a theoretical shape in the concept of *Śūnya-Puruṣa/Brahman* that was developed in the subsequent period by the five great *sant*s (Jagannātha Dāsa, Balarāma Dāsa, Acyutānanda Dāsa, Yaśovanta Dāsa and Śiśu Ananta), popularly known as Pañcasakhā. They transformed Jagannātha, the presiding deity of the land, into the symbolic representation of the ultimate metaphysical principle, viz. *Śūnya-Puruṣa/Śūnya-Brahman*. The succeeding *sant*s like Caitanya Dāsa, Arakṣita Dāsa, Dvārakā Dāsa, Divākara Dāsa, Īśvara Dāsa and others adhered to the same philosophy. Acyutānanda Dāsa's *Śūnya Saṁhitā*, *Śabda-Brahma Saṁhitā*, Balarāma Dāsa's *Virāṭa Gītā* and *Brahmāṇḍa Bhūgola*, Jagannātha Dāsa's *Tuḷa Bhiṇā*, Caitanya Dāsa's *Nirguṇa Māhātmya*, Dvārakā Dāsa's *Parace Gītā* and Arakṣita Dāsa's *Mahīmaṇḍala Gītā* developed the concept in meticulous detail.

According to Utkalīya Vaiṣṇavas the Ultimate Reality is One and unique principle. It transcends all names and forms that characterize the phenomenal world. Neither the categories of thought nor forms of speech can envelop it. It is non-conceptualizable; and thus non-graspable and ineffable in nature. Such a Reality is labelled as *Śūnya-Puruṣa*. A person's helplessness to explain this sort of Reality is best expressed in the following words of Acyutānanda Dāsa:

> Most devout persons, even gods fail to know Him. How can they? For, He is nothing. He is just Himself, for, He has no parallel. If at all we search for a parallel then He himself is his own parallel.[29]

Surprisingly, these thinkers use two apparently contradictory epithets – one Brāhmanic, viz. *Brahman* and the other non-Brāhmanic,

---

[29] Acyutānanda Dāsa, *Śabda-Brahma Saṁhitā*, I.

viz. *śūnya* – conjointly to address the same Reality. Balarāma Dāsa, one of the eminent members of the Pañcasakhā group, writes:

He has no form, no outline
He is Śūnya-Puruṣa
He is the Brahman *and the* Śūnya
How can He have a name?[30]

Like the other systems of thought that subscribes to the idea of God as *śūnya* these Vaiṣṇavas also were staunch non-dualists, and like them they believed that the world is not the product of *māyā* but the real manifestation of *Śūnya-Puruṣa*. This is evident from the following lines of Acyutānanda Dāsa:

> Right from the insects to the highest form of beings: from the inanimate to animate – all these are in His womb. All the forms and creations in this world are due to him . . . creation, existence and delusion, all these three states contained within his body. The world arises as well as dissolves here.[31]
>
> This potential womb of the entire creation is nothing but *śūnya*.[32]

Like the other *śūnya*-centric schools of thought it believed in the identity of *jīvātman* and *paramātman*. But it goes one step ahead and proclaims the identity between the individual body (*piṇḍa*) and the cosmic body (*brahmāṇḍa*), following Nātha Dharma. For it everything is permeated by the *Śūnya-Puruṣa/Brahman*. Besides, this school of thought like other *śūnya*-centric theories subscribes to the theory of *bhakti* based on the yogic realization. Despite such commonness it is easily noticeable that the Odia Vaiṣṇavas posit the concept of *Śūnya* in a wider panorama. My claim can be assessed from the following lines of Acyutānanda Dāsa, one of the pioneers

---

30 Balarāma Dāsa, *Virāṭa Gītā*, I.

31 Acyutānanda Dāsa, *Śabda-Brahma Saṁhitā*, pp. 8-12.

32 *In those days my form was* śūnya
x x x x
In my womb universe was born,
This was the manifestation of Brahman.
– Balarāma Dāsa, *Virāṭa Gītā*, I

of Utkalīya Vaiṣṇavism.

> O Vīra *look at* śūnya
> *By placing yourself in* śūnya.
> *Meditate on* śūnya,
> Śūnya *itself is the form,*
> *Ground of all discriminating knowledge.*
> *Look at the world from the pedestal of* śūnya
> *Everything arises from* śūnya *and*
> *Everything flourishes in* śūnya.
> *One may declare himself to be a* brahma-jñānī
> *But without realizing the essence of* śūnya
> *All his knowledge is but futile.*[33]

The above poem can offer us some idea of how this concept was used very pervasively. In this case not only is the Reality of the nature of *śūnya*, but also the phenomenal world of names and forms is stated to be of the same nature. The logic behind such ascription is simple. *Śūnya-Puruṣa* permeates everything. Though it has no form or shape, it is omnipresent in its creation as *Śūnya/Pūrṇa-Brahman*. The scope of *śūnya* is further extended by Jagannātha Dāsa, who declares:

> *Oṁkāra* is *parama śūnya*, all activities too are *śūnya*, all our prayers and meditations are *śūnya*, all our fancies and forms are *śūnya*.[34]

Elucidating this verse in prose he says:

> All the basic symbols of *yoga* that are used for the meditation on *Śūnya-Puruṣa*, like *bindu*, *jyoti*, *dharma* and *oṁkāra* are nothing but *śūnya*. Fifty-four letters, all *yantra* and *mantra*, *tattva* and *jñāna*, too, are *śūnya*. Even the celestial bodies such as the sun and moon are nothing but *śūnya*; also the empirical world, including the animate

---

33 Acyutānanda Dāsa, *Śūnya Saṁhitā Causaṭhī Ṭīkā*, pp. 55-57 (unpublished manuscript), MSS.O.I/617, Utkal University Library.

34 *oṁkāra parama śūnya sarvamayo karma* ।
śūnya śūnya japadhyānam sarvaśūnya matibhramam ॥
– Jagannātha Dāsa, *Tuḷa Bhiṇa*, 3.12.1 quoted in B. Mohanty, *Odia Sahityara Itihasa*, vol. I, Cuttack: Friend's Publishers, 1977, p. 278

> and inanimate beings, is in *śūnya*.[35]

It is no wonder that the *mantra* for worship is called *śūnya-mantra*. The entire idea of conceiving the modes of worship as well as the object of worship as *śūnya* appears to be curious but it is not something unusual. One may be reminded of the cryptic lines from *Prajñāpāramitā-Sūtra:* "Form is *śūnyatā* and *śūnyatā* is form." But the following lines from the Vajrayāna text *Advayavajra Saṁgraha* is closest to the above account of the Utkalīya Vaiṣṇavas:

> God who is worshipped, the worshipper who worships, the materials which are used in worship and the *mantras* of worship are nothing but *śūnya*.[36]

So the concept of *śūnya* is much more persistent in Utkalīya Vaiṣṇavism. In this case not only is the God conceived as *śūnya*, but his abode is *śūnya* and the method of self-realization is also *śūnya*. Though *Śūnya-Puruṣa/Brahman* is identified with Jagannātha, He is not to be taken as a personal God in the strictest sense of the term. Rather these philosophers display a certain amount of guts in defying the traditional tenets of Hindu theology. So they do not hesitate to dismiss all that is accepted as sacred and sacrosanct in the orthodox Hindu tradition. Even, in certain cases, their voice seems to have a non-Brāhmanical undertone. This may be evident from the following statement of Dvārakā Dāsa:

> All chantings, rituals, pilgrimages are meaningless; all the arrays of gods and goddesses are nothing but illusions.[37]

Not only these Vaiṣṇavas defy idolatry, they decry any discrimination between human beings on the basis of caste and creed. Since the divine principle *śūnya* is all-pervasive logically it follows that everybody is divine. So they preferred to identify themselves as

---

35 Jagannātha Dāsa, *Tuḷa Bhiṇa*, 3.12.1 quoted in B. Mohanty, op. cit.

36 *Advaya Vajra Saṁgraha*, quoted in N.K. Sahoo, 1958, *Buddhism in Orissa*, Bhubaneswar: Utkal University Press, p. 132.

37 *devādevī paṭala ye māyāmana tuccha* ।
– Dvārakā Dāsa, *Chhatisa Gupta Gītā*, XII

"śūdra" (the lowest caste in social heirarchy) even though they belonged to higher castes.

Another atypical dimension of Utkalīya Vaiṣṇavism is the frequent reference to Buddha. They even describe Jagannātha, the symbolic embodiment of *Śūnya-Puruṣa/Brahman*, as Buddha-Jagannātha. We also notice that in Mahimā Dharma too there is frequent reference to Buddha. Though the eminent scholars on Mahimā Dharma, including C.R. Das try not to lay a hand on the issue, it needs to be probed. But it cannot be denied that Buddhism, especially Tantric Buddhism (Vajrayāna and Sahajayāna), was assimilated with Brāhmanistic ideas in this culture.

We have so far discussed some of the systems of thought that accord the idea of *śūnya* the status of the Highest Reality. *Śūnya* in all these cases does not have a negative implication. It rather stands for the ineffability of the Absolute. So by implication all these systems contribute to non-dualism. Even Mādhyamika Buddhism which is interwoven with this concept accedes to the non-dual (*advaya*) nature of the Reality. Yet these systems of thought did not draw the idea of *śūnya* from the Mādhyamika philosophy. There was an emerging tendency for assimilation. The *śūnya*-centric metaphysics of the post-Śaṅkara phase, therefore, might be said to be a unique blending of Upaniṣadic non-dualism, Buddhism, Tantra and Yoga. The result was a unalloyed form of non-dualistic metaphysical scheme in which the distinction between God and Reality, individual self and the cosmic self, the individual body and cosmic body, and above all, the distinction between man and man on the one hand, and the man and God on the other hand, was obliterated. The pure ontology was now turned into a philosophy that was responsive to the social predicament. Therefore, there was an undertone of dissidence in all these philosophical systems, right from Kashmir Śaivism to Utkalīya Vaiṣṇavism. Mahimā Dharma, which will be the focus of this work, can be said to be more radical in its approach. Maybe its spirit of rebellion emerges from the historical and societal compulsions. But despite its radicalism, it shares the common features of the neo-metaphysical trend.

Part II

3

The Genesis of Mahimā Dharma

MAHIṂĀ Dharma may be said to be the last representative of the post-Classical Bhakti movement that came into prominence in Odisha sometime in the 1860s. That was the period when neo-Hinduism was at its peak. But unlike neo-Hinduism, Mahimā did not come into being as a reaction to Christianity or the Western critique of the Indian religion. It was very much a part of the post-Classical tradition that carried on the critique of the orthodoxy from within the larger framework Hindu Dharma. Like other protagonists of this genre Mahimā Dharma also raised its voice against social injustice and preponderance of meaningless religious practices that had become a part of our dominant Brāhmanical tradition. In the metaphysical level it followed the line of the *nirguṇa-bhakti*, popularized by the *sant*s of the post-Classical period. Rather Mahimā Dharma sailed the *nirguṇa* metaphysics to its logical conclusion. So at both the levels, viz. at the level of practice as well as the level of theory, it was uncompromisingly rebellious. As Cittaranjan Das, the famous scholar on *sant* literature very aptly points out:

> Mahimā Dharma was the last protest of the saints against the established Hindu religion. It was not a Buddhist movement, neither had it to do anything with the Vaiṣṇava way of worship. It did not believe as a religion in getting the sanction of the king to be able to survive and flourish and it proclaimed an open revolt against the externalist obsessions in religion. It flourished out of the courts, out of the influence of the king's mace, flouted the superiority of the brāhmaṇas and registered most of its followers from the lowliest and the downtrodden in society. It was an effort to give to those who stood at the lowest in a status-infested

> society, a real sense of human dignity and sought to raise them up as equals and devotees.[1]

In this chapter I intend to throw some light on the genesis of Mahimā Dharma so that I would be in a position to explore its structural and philosophical concepts more smoothly in the subsequent chapters.

The Backdrop

Odisha in the nineteenth century CE witnessed the worst form of Hindu rigidity. The faith in the caste-based structure revived with a vengeance. This was a trend that seemed quite anomalous to the general socio-cultural inclination of Odisha that had blended the multifarious philosophical forms, including Buddhism and Nāthism, in the form of a Vaiṣṇavism. This new form of Vaiṣṇavism propagated by the Odia *sant*s from fifteenth century defied the basic tenets of Brāhmanism, including the traditional caste-structures. This reversal to hardcore Brāhmanism in the subsequent phases might be ascribed to the compulsions of political situations. The century opened with the advent of the East India Company rule in 1803. Very soon the Christian missionaries followed. The Baptist Missionary Society was established at Cuttack in 1826. By 1850s Christianity had made some inroads in the land. Several publications cropped up criticizing the Jagannātha cult that for centuries had been considered to be the very basis of the Odia identity. Most probably, this evoked a sharp reaction from the conservative people of Odisha. A certain amount of insecurity made the people reinforce traditional norms of the caste hierarchy with a new vigour. This perhaps accounted for Hunter's blanket condemnation of Odias as "priest-race, kept in subjection by the brāhmaṇas and subject to all paralysing influences of religious superstition and caste prejudices. Nowhere do the caste rules exercise such an influence".[2] The Jagannātha Dharma that was considered as the unparalleled symbol of religious syncretism and

---

[1] C.R. Das, 1982, *A Glimpse into Odiya Literature*, Bhubaneswar: Orissa Sahitya Akademi, p. 157.

[2] W.W. Hunter, 1976, *A Statistical Account of Bengal*, vol. XIX, 1876, repr., Delhi: Concept Publishing Company, p. 61.

a culture of tolerance was in a quandary. One may get some hints about the state of affairs from Hunter's report in *A Statistical Account of Bengal* in 1870. He states:

> The temple of Jagannātha in which every creed obtained an asylum and in which every class and sect can find its god now closes its doors to its low-caste population.[3]

The new ordinations created fresh challenges for the people belonging to the lower strata of the society. At this point of history the king and brāhmaṇas made an unholy alliance to exclude the downtrodden and the lowly from the divine scheme of *dharma*. Such changed social stance seriously compromised Jagannātha's (the word etymologically signifies "the Lord of the universe") position as the Lord of all – high and low. This trend was quite opposed to the very spirit of Jagannātha Dharma. The *dharma* that had its roots in the aboriginal form of worship gradually absorbed within its ambit different and sometimes conflicting religious streams to finally emerge as a symbol of full-fledged religious syncretism. It embraced within its fold the elements of Brāhmanism, Buddhism, Tantra as well as some of the elements of the *savara* (aborigin) religious world-view. But during the last few decades of nineteenth century CE the circumstances led to sudden reversal to strict orthodoxism and caste-bound society. This created a great amount of frustration and agony in the mind and heart of those belonging to the lower strata of the society. Discussing about this phenomenon Ishita Banerjee-Dube rightly observes:

> The close association with royalty, coupled with the introduction of caste discrimination in practices of the temple at Purī, made Jagannātha appear in the nineteenth century as an exclusive and distant lord, a monopoly of brāhmaṇas and rulers. He had moved away far from his initial devotees and had come to be identified with those who wielded power and authority.[4]

---

[3] W.W. Hunter, op. cit., p. 62.

[4] Ishita Banerjee-Dube, 2001, "Issues of Faith, Enactment of Contest: The Founding of Mahimā Dharma in Nineteenth Century Orissa", in H. Kulke and B. Schnepel (eds.) *Jagannath Revisited: Studying Society, Religion and the State in Orissa*, New Delhi: Manohar, p. 158.

The second important factor that acted as a catalyst for the changed religious attitude of the downtrodden was the great famine of 1886. During this phase the poor people virtually starved to death and almost one-third of the population was wiped out. But what created a great consternation in the mind of such hapless people was the attitude of the rich and high regarding the strict observance of the norms of caste. They castigated the people for going against the norms of Sanātana Dharma by partaking of cooked food in relief camps (*chatra*) offered by the colonial administration. They were ostracized as *catrakhiya*s (people who have eaten in *chatra*s) and were boycotted. The problem became still acute with some administrative mismanagement. So a sense of resentment was already brewing within the society as the plight of the poor and the oppressed was getting worse day by day. All such factors created a social situation that proved to be fertile for a socio-cultural rebellion. This was the period when Mahimā Dharma appeared on the scene and soon turned into a force to reckon with.

The new *dharma* gave hope and solace to the oppressed class who badly needed a social as well as religious anchor. This was provided amply by this new *dharma* that discarded the *varṇa-vyavasthā*, i.e. caste hierarchy. Rather it excluded from its holy fold the oppressors, viz. the king as well as the brāhmaṇas. It dismissed all that stood as a symbol of Brāhmanic *dharma* including idol worship in any form. It even challenged the supremacy of Lord Jagannātha by portraying him as the disciple of Mahimā Svāmī, the founder of the new *dharma*. However, the new wave of thought that emerged in the form of Mahimā Dharma should not be portrayed as a distinct version of the reformation movement that swept different parts of India during nineteenth century CE. The new form of *dharma* did not experiment with a method of revivalism nor did it adopt the method of going back to Vedas and Upaniṣads to prove the worth of its authenticity. So there was more an element of revolution than any form of compromise.

Mahimā Svāmī

It is easy to compile the hagiography of a saint but the problems are innumerable when it comes to providing a biographical sketch of such personalities. The case of Mahimā Svāmī is no different. It is easier for the follower of a religious creed to lap up all that is provided by the hagiographers. Rather any attempt to chaff history from mystery, facts from fictions is considered to be a form of sacrilege. Such concoctions and embellishments, in fact, are essential features of the delineation of the life of a messiah/god-man. This has happened in the case of Jesus Christ, Prophet Mohammed, Guru Nānak and many others. Religion has all along been accepted as belonging to the realm of the 'other' where the role of mundane is undermined in order to yield place to the super mundane. Unless the elements of miracle and myth, mixed up godliness, cannot be thrusted upon such souls, however great they may be. We come across the same trend when we come to probe into the hagiography of Mahimā Svāmī, written by the celebrated persona of this *dharma* like Biśvanātha Bābā and Śatrughna Nāth. Though Mahimā Svāmī belonged to an age when myths could have been easily chaffed out from the facts this has not been done. Maybe this was due to the fact that very little is known about the antecedents of this great religious rebel. So to offer a purely academic account of life and actions of Mahimā Svāmī, the founder of Mahimā Dharma, is a difficult task. Yet the task must be undertaken, for without a biographical account the compulsions of the historical space cannot be understood. So I would like to rely more on the sketchy and most often scattered materials provided by newspaper reports and reports prepared by the colonial administration, however undependable and biased they might be.

Mahimā Svāmī burst into the religio-cultural scene of Odisha almost from the oblivion. The first historical account about the presence of his persona was recorded in the Odia newspaper entitled *Utkal Dipika* in its edition of 1 June 1867. It was reported that the new faith is being spearheaded by a *phalāhārī saṁnyāsī* (an ascetic surviving on fruits) in the princely states bordering the district Cuttack. According to the reports published by the British administration much later, it can be gathered that Mahimā Svāmī's original name was 'Mukunda Dāsa' (though his followers dismiss this account). Most probably, he experimented with the predominant religious trends of the period. It is reported that he spent a considerable part of his life at Purī, the seat of Jagannātha-centric Vaiṣṇavism. During this period he was known as "Dhūliā Bābā" (a mendicant smeared with dust). Next, he was seen at the Kapilās hill, the famous Śaiva centre situated at Dhenkanal district of Odisha. His sojourn at Kapilās was long. During this period he became famous as *phalāhārī bābā* and subsequently as *khīra-nīra peyī bābā* (surviving on milk and water). In all probability three descriptions coalesced together to form the personality of Mahimā Svāmī. During his stay at the Śaiva-Kṣetra Kapilās, most probably, he embraced the Śaiva faith. It has been reported that while he spent his time here he took much pain in improving the place by cutting the jungle, making gardens, looking after the sacred food of the idol, and taking care of the pilgrims who visited the hill periodically. But he emerged as the true messiah when, finally, he discarded all the traces of the traditional faith (including Vaiṣṇavism and Śaivism). He got rid of his matted locks and started wearing the bark of *kumhbī* tree (so the followers of Mahimā Dharma are also called Kumbhpaṭiās). This was the beginning of a totally new phase in his life. From a meditating mendicant he became a fire-brand preacher. One can safely presume that this great soul had an in-depth understanding of the fundamental faiths of the varied sects of Hinduism along with its dark linings. This must have given him a deep insight into what is the true essence of *dharma;* and most importantly, what was the need of the hour. Though hagiographers portray him as *ayoni sambhūta* (not born out of womb), who directly descended from Himalayas to preach a new *dharma,* one can guess that he was a local person very much in command of the local language, as his field of activity was the rural and underdeveloped parts of Odisha. He travelled extensively through the interior parts of Odisha and never thought of establishing a religious establishment in any particular place.

The *dharma* preached by Mahimā Svāmī was unique and distinct at both the levels – at the level of theory and also at the level of practice. The *dharma* projected God as the highest spiritual Being, One and unique, without form, without shape, ineffable, incomprehensible, non-scriptable (*alekha*) *Śūnya-Puruṣa*. Negatively speaking, God is non-scriptable (*alekha*) and *śūnya*; and positively speaking He can at best be described as the glorious one (*mahimā*). This might be the reason why the followers of this *dharma* are called Alekha-dharmīs and also the Mahimā-dharmīs. Such an idea of the Highest Reality might appear closest to the Upaniṣadic conception of *Brahman*. Yet in this case the complex abstraction of the Upaniṣadic *Brahman* is turned into an adorable Supreme Being, who would respond to the love and prayers of the commonest of the common. With this Mahimā Dharma did away with the well-entrenched practice of traditional idol worship. God is now portrayed as a pure spiritual being without form, yet the creator of the universe. As the creator of the universe He is all-pervading, hence equality is the keyword. In such a scheme there is no place for caste distinction or social discrimination.

At the level of practice *dharma* Mahimā Dharma, championed a life of simplicity, austerity and humility, of honesty and truthfulness, a shunning of rituals and all forms of display; and a life of total devotion. The life prescribed for the devotees suited well with the lifestyle of the poor (taking one cooked meal during the day and having no possession). This also helped the poor people to lead a life of spiritual fulfilment as they could not afford all the pomposities associated with the Brāhmanical way of religious life. Mahimā Svāmī prescribed a simple method of worshipping God under the open sky instead of going to a temple and observing the complicated methods of *pūjā* (worship) that is most often done through the mediation of a priest. The *saṁskāras* (rites) associated with birth, death, etc. which form very important part of the Hindu way of life, were dismissed as meaningless. With such new ordinances the brāhmaṇas were denied of all roles in the religious life of a Mahimā-dharmī. The defiance of the Brāhmanism is so complete that the followers of this new *dharma* are to disregard all that is considered sacred in the tradition, for example, the *tulsī* plant, regarded as the symbol of Viṣṇu is not to be touched; similarly, *mahāprasāda* (sanctified food of Lord Jagannātha) is not be considered as sacred. With such precepts and practices the new *dharma* contested the power of the brāhmaṇas, the kings and the deities.

Mahimā Svāmī established his first *tuṅgī* (place of worship) in a place called Daruthenga, in Kurda district; and began preaching his new doctrine. He made his first two disciples at Daruthenga – Govinda Dāsa and Narasiṅga Dāsa. This was the beginning of his deification and transformation into Mahimā Gosain. The new ideas and ideals spread in different directions of the state due to the efforts of his disciples. The Svāmī too travelled extensively in the tributary states preaching his new faith. What is most important is that he made it a point to feed a large number of people wherever he established his camp. That was the time of famine; and the poor and starving people were left in the lurch by the powerful and rich section of the society. Mahimā Svāmī followed a peculiar trait of burning the *tuṅgī*s (such large camps) before leaving a particular place, thereby indicating that no possessions are of any worth. A large number of family men joined the movement; and they were called *āśrita*s (protected). The order also initiated *saṁnyāsī*s, who devoted their life in spreading the message in the remote corners of the state, including the tribal areas. The new faith received unprecedented response from the large section of the poor and deprived people. These people not only considered him to be their saviour but also as the Alekha *Śūnya-Puruṣa* incarnate. We cannot confirm whether Mahimā Svāmī himself ordained his deification or not, for he left no written work. But the account provided by the manager of the State of Dhenkanal places the facts in the following way:

> I never heard from him that he professed to be the creator of the world as his disciples and followers believe him to be. From what I heard from him I concluded that the creator of the world was a spiritual Being, omnipresent and omniscient, without form,

> whom he called Mahimā and also Prabhu, and that he alone could communicate with Alekha Prabhu and get down what he wished.[5]

But after he breathed his last at Joranda of Dhenkanal district in 1876 his followers constructed a permanent establishment at the place; and this may be said to be the beginning of the process of divinization of Mahimā Gosain.

Is Mahimā Dharma Inspired by Christianity?

The immense popularity of Mahimā Dharma elicited different reactions from the people of different denominations. This may be evident from the divergent reports published in the daily *Utkal Dipika*, the mouthpiece of the traditional intelligentsia, and the report of the Baptist Missionaries of Odisha. They looked at his impact on the mass from their own angles. The initial reaction of the elites of Odisha was ambivalent; yet they could not remain complacent about the exact nature of Mahimā Svāmī's ideological leanings. The *Utkal Dipika*, that earlier had projected him as *ati nirlobha* (absolutely without greed) *saṁnyāsī*, reversed its opinion within a few years. Mahimā Svāmī was now seen as a threat to Hindu society. In its edition of 6 September 1873 the paper stated that *saṁnyāsī* and his followers were all out to destroy *jāti dharma* (caste rule). This charge was not baseless. In fact, Mahimā cult not only resisted *varṇa dharma* but also posed a serious challenge to it. Its influence was not limited within the coastal and central Odisha but extended to western Odisha also. The conversion of Bhīmā Bhoi, a poor Kandha (aboriginal) of this tract, made the much needed impact among the downtrodden. His poems were so powerful that the *dharma* started to have the general acceptance among the masses.

On the contrary, Rev. Miller, the head of the Baptist Missionary, had to offer an altogether different account of Mahimā Svāmī. He was convinced that Mahimā Dharma could pave the way for the spread of Christianity. The Mahimā Svāmī's denouncement of idolatry and ritualism was thought to be close to the Christian ways. So Rev. Miller came to the conclusion that Mahimā Dharma was

---

[5] Ishita Banerjee-Dube, op. cit., p. 155.

inspired by Christianity. He reported:

> He (Mahimā Svāmī) was very reserved as to his former history, when and where he got hold of his present views. It seems he lived near Choga some years ago, and there had several interviews with the native preacher. This may account for some of his ideas.[6]

It was hoped that the new religious doctrine would lead its followers on the path of Christianity. This is evident from Rev. Miller's remark that Mahimā Svāmī's teachings have induced "whole villages to give up idolatry as far as the worship of village idols is concerned". He felt that this movement is "destined to have an important bearing on the spread of Christianity in *garjats*".[7] Whether Mahimā Svāmī was influenced by Christianity or not is a matter of wild guess. But still some Western scholars toy with this presupposition.[8] However, the dismissal of idol worship and adhering to monotheism (if monotheism and non-dualism are taken to be equivalent) are not something unknown to the Indian philosophico-religious tradition. Coming to the cultural ambience of Odisha, one may notice that, these ideas were not also totally alien to the land. Odia *sant* philosophers right from fifteenth century have harped on non-idolatry,[9] non-dualism and social equality as the basic presuppositions of their religious world-view. Besides, it should be carefully noted that Mahimā Dharma, though non-conformist, never claimed itself to be an "outsider". This is evident from the

---

6 The Indian Misssionary Report on Orissa Baptist Mission for 1873-74, Baptist Missionary Society Archives, Angus Library, Regent's Park, Oxford. Quoted in Ishita Banerjee-Dube, op. cit., p. 156.

7 Ibid.

8 See A. Eschmann, 1978, "Mahimā Dharma: An Autochthonous Reform Movement of Orissa", in H. Kulke and G.C. Tripathi (eds.), *The Cult of Jagannath and the Regional Traditions of Orissa*, New Delhi: Manohar, p. 384.

9 Dwaraka Dāsa, the seventeenth-entury Odia philosopher-poet dismissing idolatry says, "All these arrays of gods and goddesses are but mere illusions" (*Parace Gītā*, III).

following lines of Sant Bhīmā Bhoi, who was often ostracized by the orthodox society as spreading the message of Christianity:

For preaching you as the indescribable one,
They mock me as a Christian
And put me to untold sufferings.[10]

The conviction that Mahimā Dharma is actually a regional version of Christianity is so deep-rooted among certain section of religious preachers that even after a hundred years of its emergence the opinion to some extent remains unaltered.[11] But there should not be any doubt in the minds of the scholars of Mahimā Dharma regarding its traditional affiliation. The four theoretical pillars of the Indian religious and philosophical tradition – the transitory nature of *saṁsāra*, law of *karma*, rebirth and *mokṣa* as the final goal of human life – form the very basis of Mahimā Dharma too.

Some scholars have hinted at the Buddhist and Jaina affiliation of Mahimā Dharma. I would like to take up the issue in detail in the Appendix while dealing with their philosophical position.

Bhīmā Bhoi: The Vanguard Mahimā Literature

One of the important contributions of Mahimā Svāmī to the enrichment of philosophical literature of Orissa was the conversion of Bhīmā Bhoi, a simple Kandha (tribal) to the Mahimā Dharma. Whatever we know of Mahimā Dharma is through the writings of this great poet-philosopher. His role becomes crucial in view of the fact that Mahimā Svāmī had no written works; and all those *siddha*s whom Mahimā Svāmī had chosen to preach the new *dharma* had also no written works. So what is left for the posterity is the voluminous literature handed down by the *sant*-poet Bhīmā Bhoi. His works were virtually treated as the holy scripture of Mahimā Dharma and even to day sung by the Mahimāites, though certain

---

10 *Stuti-Cintāmaṇi*, 20th *bolī*.

11 See Johannes Beltz, 2003, " Bhīmā Bhoi: The Making of a Modern Saint", in A. Copley (ed.), *Hinduism in Public and Private: Reform, Hindutva, Gender and Sampradaya*, New Delhi: Oxford University Press.

sections of its followers underplay his role as a true mouthpiece of this new religio-philosophical order. For quite some time he was often identified with the founder of *dharma*. His role was not limited to the enrichment of Mahimā Dharma alone.

> Bhīmā Bhoi is the precious gift of Mahimā Dharma to Odiya literature and he should also be claimed as the most precious gift of Orissa and Odiya literature to the legacy that is India.[12]

Even *Utkal Dipika*, that often portrayed Mahimā Dharma in adverse light, almost grudgingly admits, "His compositions are of rare merit and even educated people can seldom compose like him."[13] He represents Orissa's contribution to the Indian cultural heritage. For instance, when the Sahitya Akademi asked for a poetic passage from each of the fourteen Indian languages, a couplet of Bhīmā Bhoi's *Stuti-Cintāmaṇi* was chosen.[14]

Bhīmā Bhoi, though born only 150 years back, still continues to be more mysterious and enigmatic figure in Odishan history than perhaps his preceptor Mahimā Gosain. His powerful literary works as well as the interesting anecdotes that abound about him refuse to dim despite the passage of time. They are mind-bogglingly divergent. If the census report prepared by the administration in 1911 ascribes him to the role of the chief instigator of the attack on Jagannātha Temple at Purī, then some modern scholars project him as the voice of the subaltern and the underprivileged. If a certain section of researchers love to project him as a man of loose morals, a "lady killer" and a sort of transvestite, then a considerable section of population of Odisha consider him as the saviour and a god-man.[15] Controversies and debates are aplenty about Bhīmā Bhoi's blindness. Scholars love to invent the story that this genius was not a tribal man but a brāhmaṇa by birth, raised by a tribal couple. In

---

12 C.R. Das, *A Glimpse into Oriya Literature*, p. 158.

13 *Utkal Dipika* (daily newspaper), 19 November 1881.

14 *mo jībana pachhe narke padi thāu jagata uddhāra heu* ।
(Let my life be condemned to hell, but let the world be uplifted.)

15 See Johannes Beltz, "Bhīmā Bhoi: The Making of a Saint".

the last decade there has been a spurt of research publications on this man that concentrate more on hagiography than on unravelling facts about the life of this genius. This also partly explains why all the attempts to construct a biography of Bhīmā Bhoi are almost impossible for all factual details about him are lost in the shrouds of hagiography and legends. Of course, in his literature one comes across certain biographical undertone. But whether we can call them "authentic" or not is a matter of serious doubt. The meagre documents available on him should not be taken as the conclusive evidence but narratives of truth. From all these materials we can construct a brief biographical sketch of Bhīmā Bhoi.

Bhīmā Bhoi was born sometime between CE 1845 and 1855. There is a lot of controversy about his birthplace, but this is at least clear that he did not hail from the prosperous coastal Odisha but from the western Odisha. It is also true that he belonged to the Kandha community, a tribal group of the western Odisha. There should not be any unnecessary controversy about his tribal origin for he has all along claimed to be Kandha in the colophones of most of his poems. The controversy seems to stem from certain baffling and inexplicable facts. First and foremost, the question that is likely to haunt any serious scholar is – how could an illiterate Kandha compose such powerful verses on very abstract and intricate philosophical system? Besides, the language he used was more in tune with the philosophical literature of the coastal district rather than the dialect used in the western part of Odisha. Is it not a matter of mystery? The staunch followers of Mahimā Dharma ascribe this to the blessings of his Guru Mahimā Svāmī. But from the biographical references in his compositions it might not be difficult to guess that the man was endowed with tremendous poetic power and perhaps well known in his locality. This might be the foremost reason why Mahimā Svāmī chose him to be the poetic messenger of the new *dharma*. Besides, as per his own admission, he spent his childhood as a cowherd in an orthodox family where he took keen interest in listening to *Bhāgavata* composed by Jagannātha Dāsa, one of the prominent members of the Pañcasakhā group of *sants*. The recitation from Jagannātha Dāsa's composition was a regular phenomenon in the villages. It appears that along with his poetic powers Bhīmā Bhoi must have been endowed with extraordinary memory. This helped him to compose philosophical verses almost in tune with phraseology and style of the *sant* predecessors (sixteenth century CE). Whatever it may be, the influence of the indigenous Odia *sant* literature is more than conspicuous in Bhīmā Bhoi's works as far as the style and content are concerned. They are so close to the literature of the indigenous Odia Vaiṣṇavas popularly known as Pañcasakhā that it leaves one with the impression that Bhīmā Bhoi was a true successor of the Odia *sant* tradition.

If we go by Bhīmā Bhoi's admission then it appears that his initiation into Mahimā Dharma happened quite early in his life. It seems that he was initiated into the *dharma* by its founder around 1862. By the age of 16 he had acquired considerable prominence within the Mahimāite community on account of his devotional compositions that were first sung at the Mahimā Dharma convention at Khuntuni in 1865 (Biśvanātha Bābā 1957; 1978). During this phase of his career Bhīmā met his important disciples and life-long companions – Hari Panda and Basudev Panda. They acted as his scribes. However, as an ardent follower of his *guru* and the protagonist of Mahimā Dharma, his life was not that easy. His views were already recognized as a threat to the orthodox society. He had to face the wrath of the public as well as powerful rulers from time to time. What added to his woe was his forced distancing from the mainstream Mahimā movement after the death of Mahimā Svāmī. This was most probably due to his status as a family man. He was not only married but had more than one wife. Another fact that created such estrangement was his stature as a god-man among the tribal and low-caste people of western Odisha. So he migrated from one place to another till he could finally settle at Khaliāpallī of Sonepur district in 1877. He composed voluminous literature on the philosophical aspects of Mahimā Dharma, viz. *Stuti-Cintāmaṇi*, *Brahma-Nirūpaṇa Gītā*, *Nirveda Sādhanā*, *Mahimā Binoda*, *Aṣṭaka-Bihārī Gītā*, *Śrutiniṣedha Gītā* and more than 300 short poems in the form of *bhajanas* (paeans to Lord). Some of his works are not yet published. He not only wrote in Odia but also in Bengali and Ledia (a mixture of Hindi, Bengali and Odia). Though his works in other languages are not that perfect, perhaps they were good enough for spreading the message of Mahimā Dharma in the neighbouring states like Bengal, Bihar and Assam. He died at a comparatively young age (45 years) in 1895.

I have provided perhaps the briefest biographical account of two great pivots of Mahimā Dharma – the rebellious spiritual leader who provided a new meaning to *dharma,* Mahimā Svāmī, and his able disciple, Bhīmā Bhoi, who was largely responsible for keeping the message of a novel faith alive in the academic as well as non-academic circles.

The Tenets of Mahimā Dharma

Before I take up a full-fledged discussion on the philosophical foundations of Mahimā Dharma I would like to present in a nutshell the basic tenets of this *dharma*:

- Mahimā Dharma believes that there is but one and unique Reality who has been often addressed as *Śūnya-Brahman* and *Alekha,* as this reality is conceived to be ineffable transcending all the categories of conceptualization and thought. Thus they describe it with all possible negative predicates like *alekha, arūpa, adṛśya, anirdeśya, anakṣara, avyakta, anāma, adeha, nirupādhi, nirvikalpa, nirañjana* and *nirvikāra*. But even if ineffable, He is the object of devotion (*bhakti*). The only positive predicate applied is Mahimā (glorious, the powerful one).
- The Mahimā Dharma does not believe in idol worship, sacramental rituals, all sorts of superstitions perpetrated in the name of religion. The only rite permitted is of *śaraṇa* (taking refuge in) and *darśana* (having the view of) in Mahimā. This must be performed seven times before the sunrise by turning towards the east; and again five times in the evening before the sunset by turning the face towards the west. It consists

of complicated physical postures something akin to *sūrya-namaskāra* accompanied by the utterance of the word *alekha*. Though admitting the existence of God, it discards all forms of idolatry.

- Though ineffable and non-qualified, *Śūnya-Brahman* is regarded as the manifest cause of the universe. The visible universe is the manifestation of the *mahimā* (glory) of *Parama Brahman*. All the things of the world are illuminated and made conscious due to the direction of the conscious Almighty. He is the creator of everything – animate and inanimate. So He is all-pervading and permeates through all his creations. In this sense he is *vibhu*.
- As uncompromising non-dualists they believe that there is no distinction between the creation and the world; and between the individual soul (*jīva)* and the universal soul, i.e. *parama*. Since *Parama Brahman* is all-pervasive there is no distinction between man and man. There is but one caste, that is the caste of humanity. So serving God implies service to the humanity.
- Mahimā Dharma lays emphasis on *bhakti* as a mode of spirituality. Though it highlights on *bhakti, bhakti* for its followers is not just an unconditional surrender to God; it is something more than this. The true knowledge is a precondition to *bhakti*. This is known as *jñāna-bhakti*. Realizing the ephemeral nature of the life one should always be engaged in the pursuit of *ātma-jñāna* (self-knowledge) and *tattva-jñāna* (knowledge of the ultimate truth). It emphasizes the importance of meditation and a life of dedication as the path to liberation. The path often highlighted is that of truth, forgiveness, non-violence and peace. As an object of *bhakti*, the Highest Reality, is sometimes addressed as *dayāmaya* (embodiment of kindness), *sarvāntaryāmī* (omniscient) and *jñāna-bhakti-dātā* (endower of *jñāna* and *bhakti*).
- One of the important features of Mahimā Dharma is its strong ethical undertone. The principal ethical commandments are:

worship no idol, do not kill, do not eat meat, do not lie, do not steal, do not commit adultery, follow the directions for the sexual behaviour in marriage, exercise propriety, goodwill and kindness towards all creatures. Added to this are a series of drastic commandments like accept no food from the brāhmaṇas, take nothing after sunset and take bath every morning before prayer.

- Since these commandments demand a very rigorous life there are different grades within the initiated. The highest in the hierarchy are called *balkaladhārī*s, who wear the bark of *kumbhī* tree, the *kanapaṭiā*s, the second in the order wear the loin-clothes. These two classes of the initiated lead the life of *saṁnyāsī*. The householders (*gr̥h-bhakta*s) are placed next to the other two groups. The codes of the *dharma* are more lenient for them. All *saṁnyāsī*s are expected to stick to three norms, i.e. to work for the welfare of the *gādī* (institution), for the welfare of the community and for the welfare of the entire world.

4

God as Śūnya: Mahimā Dharma

We have already scanned the major philosophical systems that adhere to a unique metaphysical position which ascribes ineffability to the Highest Reality, even if the principle is most often identified with either a god of the Brāhmanic tradition (Śiva or Viṣṇu) or of Buddhist tradition (Vajrasattva). Another name for the ineffability of this ultimate principle is *śūnya*. Now I take up for discussion the main theme of this work, viz. *śūnya* in Mahimā Dharma, that refuses to symbolize God through any name, orthodox or unorthodox. Metaphysically speaking it advocates unalloyed non-dualism (Advaitavāda). In the case of Mahimā Dharma the metaphysical principles play a greater role in the absence of its conspicuous theistic leanings. Therefore, in its scheme of *dharma* there is no God existing either in the heaven or inside a temple. God is *Alekha, Śūnya-Brahman/Puruṣa*, nameless, formless, inconceivable being. In other words, God is of the nature of *Śūnya-Brahman* or *Puruṣa*. Its metaphysical structure as well as practical philosophy rests on this concept. The entire range of its attitude to *dharma* as well as to life is but a logical conclusion to the basic premise that God is of the nature of *śūnya*. In this chapter I intend to concentrate on the explication of this concept from all possible angles.

Before I spell out the philosophical position of Mahimā Dharma and its stand on the theory of God as *śūnya* let me make it clear in no uncertain terms that like many other scholars[1] I believe that Mahimā philosophy is a continuation of the medieval philosophical tradition of Odisha. One cannot deny the strong impact of the

[1] S.C. Panigrahi 1992; Bettina Bäumer 2010; A. Eschmann 1986; Nepak 1997; Siddhartha Das 2001; Mahtāb 1961.

Utkalīya Vaiṣṇavas who preached a philosophy that can be said to be a unique syncretism of Tantric Buddhism, Nātha Dharma and Yoga. The basic philosophical concepts of Mahimā Dharma are drawn from the philosophical ideas floated by the five great *sant*s (Pañcasakhā) who flourished during sixteenth century and also Caitanya Dāsa, another contemporary *sant*. It is very difficult to dismiss their influence. Of course, the influential section of Mahimā-panthīs has persistently dismissed this claim since 1930s especially after Avadhūta Biśvanātha Bābā overshadowed the sect with his highly Sanskritized interpretation of the Mahimā ideology. According to them this *dharma* has nothing to do with any form of regional philosophy, especially Utkalīya Vaiṣṇavism.

I would like to counter this claim on two grounds. First and foremost, it has been alleged that the Odia medieval *sant*s were Vaiṣṇavas and Mahimā Dharma is opposed to any allegiance to any sectarian God (in this case Viṣṇu). But it should be noted that one of the uncharacteristic features of Odia popular culture is the indiscriminate use of the word *vaiṣṇava*. In Odia religio-philosophical tradition the word *vaiṣṇava* does not necessarily mean "the sectarian worshippers of Viṣṇu"; otherwise the Odia *sant*s, who did not strictly follow the basic presumptions of Vaiṣṇavism, in general, would not have been designated as Vaiṣṇavas. In this context what is most significant is the use of the word *vaiṣṇava* by Bhīmā Bhoi. I cite here one such example. He writes:

He brought me out from my birth place
And initiated me into Vaiṣṇavism. (emphasis mine)[2]

Here the verse with biographical undertone refers to his initiation into Mahimā Dharma by his *guru*, viz. Mahimā Svāmī. Again, at many places he uses the expression "Vaiṣṇava" to refer to his *guru.*[3] None of the *siddha*s of Mahimā Dharma has contested the use of the term *vaiṣṇava* by Bhīmā Bhoi. We must therefore assume that the word has a typical colloquial use. Most probably it meant a form of non-

---

[2] *Stuti-Cintāmaṇi*, 64th bolī.

[3] *Stuti-Cintamaṇi*, 23, 29; *Bhajanamālā*, I.55, 66.

orthodox religious position that defies caste and creed distinction.[4] At the same time, we must be cautious enough not to read unrelated meanings to the word.[5] While referring to the close affinity between the philosophical stance of Bhīmā Bhoi and the Utkalīya Vaiṣṇavas, one may note that though these groups of the Odia medieval *sant*s were self-acclaimed Vaiṣṇavas they defied the Vaiṣṇava philosophy and theology by delineating God as *Nirguṇa-Śūnya-Puruṣa*.

Second, when we come to the specific notion of God as *Alekha*, *Śūnya-Brahman* or *mahimā*, we can validly presume that the idea has not suddenly emerged from a Sanskritized tradition, as has been claimed by a powerful section of Mahimāites. The poor, illiterate people from the lower rung of the society who were initially the adherents of Mahimā Dharma had no access to such sophisticated and the so-called sacred texts. Such people, who were the real adherents of this non-orthodox religio-philosophy were most likely influenced by the texts and orally circulated ideas already written in the language of the people. So there is no wonder that in content and the use of language there is a close similarity between the medieval

[4] There is a popular saying in Odia that twelve *jātis* (castes) and thirteen creeds lose all significance once a person embraces Vaiṣṇavism.

[5] Interestingly, some modern scholars take the word *vaiṣṇava* in literal sense and present a very misconstrued idea about Bhīmā Bhoi as well as Mahimā Svāmī. Johannes Beltz (*Hinduism in Public and Private*, 2003: 234) and S. Satpathy (2006: 28) without any authentication bring in the idea of Radhābhāva of Gauḍīya Vaiṣṇavism and state that Mahimā Svāmī and Bhīmā Bhoi "form a couple like Kṛṣṇa and Rādhā". With such a fanciful presentation they wanted to justify the use of *Vaiṣṇava* in Mahimā literature. Is it not an irony that when an influential section of scholars (K. Kara, *Bhaktakabi Bhīmā Bhoi Granthavali*, pp. 41-43) even resist the very idea that Mahimā Dharma was impacted by Odia medieval philosophical tradition on the ground that it is a form of Vaiṣṇavism, how could one imagine of putting Mahimā Dharma within the scheme of Gauḍīya Vaiṣṇavism? Such fanciful delineations might lead to a great injustice to Mahimā Dharma and its founder Mahimā Svāmī. Bhīmā Bhoi never expresses any form of eroticism or romanticism while referring to his *guru*, Mahimā Svāmī.

Odia philosopher-poets and a staunch Mahimāite like Bhīmā Bhoi. The *bhajana*s of the Pañcasakhā were equally popular amongst the common mass of the period. My claim would be clearly evident as we proceed with the analysis of the key philosophical concepts of Mahimā Dharma.

Alekha and Mahimā

Before I move on to explicate the Mahimā conception of God let me dwell briefly on two keywords that form the very identity of this system of thought, viz. *alekha* and *mahimā*.

The term *alekha* is so frequently used in Mahimā literature that the followers of this *dharma* are also known in Odisha as Alekhiās. Much confusion persists about the word. If we follow the tradition truly then the term should mean "non-scriptable". This suits the Mahimā stand on the nature of the Absolute, i.e. it is beyond words and concepts – *alekha Para-Brahman*. Unfortunately, the word *alekha* that forms the very quintessence of the Mahimā faith has often been confused with the word *alakha* (invisible); and on the basis of such misinterpretation Mahimā-panthīs are taken to be a sect of Alakhanāmīs.[6] Lal Dêd, the famous *sant* of Kashmir popularized the sect. Primarily the word *alakha* is the Sanskrit equivalent of the term *alaksya* (invisible one). This distinction in the significance of the terms *alakha* and *alekha* is most often missed. So an eminent scholar like S.B. Dasgupta concludes that the word *alekha* should signify invisible one.[7] He also feels that Nānak also preached the religion of *alekha*. But it is a sheer distortion of truth. Nānak uses the word of *akāl* (timeless), not *alekha*. Even if the word is used it is used in the sense of *alakha*. Such confusion is also noted in Hastings *Encyclopedia of Religion and Ethics*.[8] According to this text the "Alakhiyā", the

---

[6] Ksitimohan Sen, "The Medieval Mystics of North India", *The Cultural Heritage of India*, vol. IV, Calcutta: The Ramkrishna Mission Institute of Culture, p. 390.

[7] S.B. Dasgupta, *Obscure Religious Cults*, pp. 351 and 360.

[8] Grierson (1908: 276) referred in *Verses from the Void*, ed. Bettina Bäumer and Johannes Beltz, Delhi: Manohar, 2010, p. 42.

"follower of unseeable" is the name of a group of sects in India "who have tenets much in common, based on the central idea that the Supreme Deity is incomprehensible or as they say 'unseeable'. What is commonly followed in such sects is the practice of calling out *alakh*." But this is a case of gross misrepresentation of the fact. The followers of Mahimā *pantha* use the word *alekha mahimā para-Brahma*. In this case *alekha* exclusively means "non-writable" or "non-scriptable". The term is the negative expression of the root *likh* (writing). This is evident from the following lines of the *sant*-philosopher Bhīmā Bhoi.

> In the four *yugas* (aeons) the poets failed to write about him
> So they named Him as *alekha*.[9]

Again,

> It is impossible to write about *Alekha Puruṣa*, (so) who can describe him?[10]

It should be noted that the word *alekha*, in no sense, is a new coinage by Mahimā Svāmī. The term was in use long before Mahimā Dharma evolved. The famous Odia *sant*, Caitanya Dāsa, who preceded Bhīmā Bhoi also interprets the term with same implication:

> As all attempts to describe it in written words failed, so it acquired the name *alekha*.[11]

Explicating it further he says:

> Who on earth can complete its description in written words, since it has no beginning or end. Such is the *mahimā* (glory) of *Alekha Puruṣa*. All acts of *śūnya* happen in the *śūnya* alone.[12]

---

[9] *cāriyuge kabi lekhina pārile* ।
alekha boliṇa nāma tahun dele ॥ — *Bhajanamālā*, II.178

[10] *alekh puruṣa nāma lekhi na hui* ।
kehun pāriba kahi ॥ — *Bhajanamālā*, I.79

[11] *lekhā karanteṇa yeṇu samāpta na hoila* ।
alekha boli teṇu nāma se bahilā ॥ — *Viṣṇugarbha Purāṇa*, 4th canto

[12] Ibid., 3rd canto.

In fact, the word *alekha* has a long history in the religio-philosophical literature of Odisha. The earliest treatise where we come across the term is *Śiśu Veda*, a thirteenth-century Nātha treatise written in archaic Odia. It says:

> It was born in *śūnya* and had its death in *śūnya*, but had a glimpse of *alekha*.[13]

Similarly, *Amarakośa*, another work of this order, mentions the word very frequently. I quote one such verse here:

> Tie yourself with the rope of *alekha*, no enemy can enter your house.[14]

So we must note two important facts here, first, Alekha Dharma alias Mahimā Dharma is distinct from all other forms of *dharma*s based on the conception of *alakha* (invisible god); second, the tradition of referring to God as *alekha* (non-scriptable) is deeply rooted in Odia religio-philosophical tradition. This is an expression of negative predication that finally signifies the ineffability and indescribability of the Absolute Reality.

If the word *alekha* is a case of negative predication then the word *mahimā* is a case of positive attribution. The only predicate that can represent the non-attributable reality is the word *mahimā*. In fact, the new *dharma* takes its name after this word. The word *mahimā* etymologically signifies (*mahata* + *ramaṇa*) glory, eternal, truth, the highest one, the divine. Again, this word is also not a new coinage. One comes across the use of the term in *Yajurveda Prapāṭhaka*, *Muṇḍaka*, *Kaṭha* and *Śvetāśvatara Upaniṣad*s, *Bhāgavatam*, *Viṣṇu Purāṇa*, etc. However, in Hindu religion, God is seldom addressed as *mahimā*. But such use is quite common in the *bhakti* philosophy of Odisha. Acyutānanda Dāsa, the eminent Pañcasakhā philosopher and the author of *Śūnya Saṁhitā*, uses the term with reference to the Highest Reality. He declares:

> Those who take resort to *mahimā* have no fear of danger, this I

---

13 *Śiśu Veda*, ed. B. Mohanty, p. 80.

14 *Amarakośa*, 2nd *paṭala*, Manuscript collected by N. Pradhan.

> have heard directly from the Lord.[15]

Again in another powerful philosophical treatise entitled *Śūnya Saṁhitā Causaṭhī Ṭīkā*, Acyutānanda Dāsa uses the word *mahimā* as a synonym of the Absolute Reality:

> *O courageous man! Take resort to* mahimā
> *He has expressed himself as the potential form in the* mahāśūnya.[16]

Thus the people of Odisha were very much acquainted with the word *mahimā*. This is the reason why the common and non-elite population of Odisha, that formed the main base of this new form of *dharma*, could grasp the essence of faith that addresses God as *mahimā–alekha*. As is well known, a large section of our populace, including śūdras and women, people belonging to the so-called untouchable class, etc. was denied access to Vedas and Upaniṣads. So it seems an incongruous claim to say that the idea of *mahimā* was straight away lifted from the Śāstras as has been claimed by some scholars. To understand the implication of the concept of *mahimā* the ordinary mass who followed this faith needed some acquaintance with this rather sophisticated idea. Since the idea was already ingrained in the culture through popular works of the Nātha *yogīs* and the unorthodox Vaiṣṇavas of Odisha, the new form of *dharma* could become a part of the life of common people.

God as Śūnya

Like many eminent systems of thought discussed in Chap. 2, Mahimā Dharma too conceives God as *śūnya*. But there are certain basic differences between these systems of thought and Mahimā Dharma as expounded in the works of Bhīmā Bhoi. In this case the word *śūnya* is used not sporadically but profusely while explicating its philosophical position. Most significantly the term *śūnya* is used with much wider implications than any other system of thought, the only exception being the philosophical literature of the Utkalīya Vaiṣṇava.

---

15 Acyutānanda Dāsa, *Śūnya Saṁhitā*, 23rd canto.

16 B. Mohanty, quoted from an unpublished manuscript, Utkal University Library, referred earlier, p. 86.

Bhīmā Bhoi in his philosophy-oriented treatises, *Brahma-Nirūpaṇa Gītā* and *Śrutiniṣedha Gītā* and in his collection of *bhajanas*, quite frequently uses the word *śūnya* with reference to the highest reality. In fact, his work *Brahma-Nirūpaṇa Gītā* starts with the prayer to the Almighty as *śūnya śūnya mahāśūnya alekha puruṣa*. Similarly, while eulogizing the Lord Supreme in his work *Śrutiniṣedha Gītā* he writes:

> Hail O *Mahāśūnya-Brahman*! who is beyond all desires, attachments and predication . . . .[17]

Now it is obvious that he conceives the Highest Reality as *śūnya*. But interestingly, he uses the word with wider implications. Not only is God of the nature of *śūnya*, He is even said to be the embodiment of *śūnya* (*śūnya-dehī*);[18] He roams in *śūnya* (*śūnya vihāra*);[19] and again his abode (*śūnya mandira*) is *śūnya* and he resides in *śūnya* (*śūnyavāsī*). Then moving one step ahead Bhīmā Bhoi claims *śūnya* as the potential womb from which the creation proceeds. Even the creation is said to emerge from the sound that is of the nature of *śūnya*. These verses indicate that Bhīmā Bhoi uses the word *śūnya* with limitless implications. So I quote some verses from the works of Bhīmā Bhoi so that we can be in a position to grasp the depth of the concept of God as *śūnya*.

> *He roams in the* śūnya, *his footsteps*
> *You fathom within your heart.*
> *Limitless is the ocean called* mahimā.[20]
>
> *He has neither form nor outline*
> *The* śūnya-*bodied has appeared in the* śūnya.[21]
>
> *He has neither form nor a contour*
> *Whose abode is the temple of* śūnya.

---

[17] *Śrutinisedha Gītā*, 1.

[18] *Bhajanamālā*, I.53.

[19] Ibid., I.7.

[20] Ibid., I.5.

[21] Ibid., I.53.

Do not talk of duality
Take recourse to the One and Unique.[22]

From the verses quoted above one must not conclude that *śūnya* is a fanciful epithet for Mahimā Dharma. *Śūnya* is rather seen as an all-pervasive principle. One may be reminded here of the famous lines of Jagannātha Dāsa, one of the eminent members of the Pañcasakhā group of Utkalīya Vaiṣṇavism.

> *Oṁkāra* is *Parama-Śūnya*, all our activities too are *śūnya*. All prayers and meditations are *śūnya*, all forms and fancies are *śūnya*.[23]

Further:

> . . . Even the celestial bodies like sun and moon are nothing but *śūnya*; and also the empirical world, including the animate and inanimate beings, is in *śūnya*.[24]

Here we find that the word *śūnya* has a wide canvas. It has been used in such a pervasive sense at least three centuries prior to the rise of Mahimā Dharma. Therefore we cannot say that Bhīmā Bhoi uses the word *śūnya* just as a non-connotative appellation of God. The word has some real significance for him. If we go by the etymological significance of the word *śūnya* then it may mean "void", "emptiness", "nothing-ness". But Bhīmā Bhoi would not prefer to delineate God as void or nothingness. Then what does the term really signify? In his famous work *Nirveda Sādhanā* Bhīmā Bhoi categorically states: "*Brahman* is nothing but *mahāśūnya*."[25]

Now we find that Bhīmā Bhoi identifies *śūnya* with *Brahman*. We have discussed earlier that there is virtually no connotative incongruity between these two words – *śūnya* and *Brahman*. In other *śūnya*-centric metaphysical systems like Kashmir Śaivism both the words – *Brahman* and *śūnya* – are used to address the Highest Reality,

---

22 *Bhajanamālā*, I.53.

23 Jagannātha Dāsa, *Tuḷa Bhiṇā*, III.12.1.

24 Ibid.

25 *brahmaku mahāśūnya kahi* ।
– *Nirveda Sādhanā*, 5th canto

viz. Parama-Śiva. But in the case of Bhīmā Bhoi or for that matter the medieval Vaiṣṇava philosophers of Odisha, both the words are used conjointly, viz. *Śūnya-Brahman,* though sometimes they are used interchangeably.[26] But that is not the end of such syncretic connotation; Bhīmā Bhoi also identifies these two terms with *pūrṇa.*

The indivisible Brahman *is One and unique*
He lacks nothing as he is self-complete (pūrṇa).
This is what is called as śūnya *and* mahāśūnya,
Nothing transcends Him.[27]

He again reiterates that *śūnya* is nothing less than *pūrṇanāda* and *Pūrṇa-Brahman.*[28]

Here we notice that in Bhīmā Bhoi's works three key concepts – *śūnya, Brahman* and *pūrṇa* – as if coalesce together to represent the Highest Reality. We have discussed in the previous chapter how *śūnya* truly signifies not the emptiness or void but self-completeness (*pūrṇa*). When a principle is self-complete no addition or attributes can enhance its value. It rather resists all kinds of predication, categorization and conceptualization. In brief, in this case the highest reality signifies pure and simple ineffability of the Reality Supreme. So Bhīmā Bhoi says:

Beyond word he is, and beyond thought
His body is śūnya
Who can find him in the scriptures?
Who can find him in the thought or form?[29]

Bhīmā Bhoi does not find any incongruity in such atypical use. For

---

[26] It has no shape or colour, it is invisible without a name.
This *brahman* is called *Śūnya-Brahman.*

nāhi tāhāra rūpa rekha । *adṛśya avarṇa tā cinha* । *tāku brahma boli kahi* । *śūnya brahmati se bolāi* । – Achyutānanda Dāsa, *Brahma Saṁhitās,* IV

[27] *Brahma-Nirūpaṇa Gītā,* 3rd canto.

[28] *pūrṇānanda pūrṇabrahma aṭanti sehi* । *cinha tāhānku dhyāyī* ।।
– *Bhajanamālā* I.68

[29] *Stuti-Cintāmaṇi,* 46th *bolī.*

him these words have the same connotation. This is evident from Bhīmā Bhoi's definition of the word *Brahman*, viz. *Brahman* is nothing but *mahāśūnya*. Such a definition is also to be found in the medieval philosophical literature of the land. For example, Acyutānanda Dāsa, the sixteenth-century philosopher, says:

> *It has no shape, no colour*
> *It is invisible and without a name.*
> *This* Brahman *is called* Śūnya-Brahman.[30]

The use of the term *śūnya* in consonance with *Brahman* was so common in Odishan culture that neither the common man nor the philosophers of the land who wrote their philosophy for this segment of the populace were aware of the fact that these two words – *Brahman* and *śūnya* – are drawn from the two so-called inimical tradition, Brāhmanical and non-Brāhmanical, respectively. Does not the combination of the concepts – *śūnya* and *Brahman* – sound a little queer, since no other philosophical or religious tradition of India uses these two terms conjointly? One may ask: why did Bhīmā Bhoi, for that matter his predecessors, append the word *Brahman* to *śūnya*? One of them has its roots in the Buddhist tradition and the other one is the Vedic/Upaniṣadic tradition. It seems that there existed a distinct philosophical tradition in Odisha that did not view these two concepts as originating from rival metaphysical sources.[31] This fusion also proves that the ideas of *śūnya* and *Brahman* are not extracted directly either from Buddhism or from Advaitism. However, at certain places Eschmann claims that Mahimā Dharma takes up "the Buddhist concept of emptiness (*śūnya*) and identifies with the Hindu conception of *Parama-Brahman* and *Īśvara-Puruṣa*".[32]

---

30 Acyutānanda Dāsa, *Śabda-Brahma Saṁhitā*, 4th canto.

31 Eschmann (1978) rightly points out about this fusion of cultures. I entirely agree with her that Mahimā Dharma has its roots in the medieval Vaiṣṇava tradition of Odisha, a Vaiṣṇavic tradition that defied all the philosophical norms of Vaiṣṇavism.

32 Eschmann (1978: 389). Though in the next lines she admits the role of the Odia medieval *sant*s in the development of Mahimā Dharma.

But such presuppositions may be misleading. We must not forget that *śūnya* does not mean "emptiness" as this has been made clear by Bhīmā Bhoi while identifying *śūnya* with *pūrṇa*. Such sweeping interpretations may prove to be counter-effective as we must realize that the tradition built around the concept of *Śūnya-Puruṣa* is not so uncomplicated. It must have taken ages to arrive at such a form of syncretism. Odisha was fortunate in the sense that diverse and variegated systems of thought had left their footprints on the land. All these strands of thought could not sustain their individuality for long. They finally got amalgamated with the other philosophical trends to form a grand synthesis. Some strands of Tantric Buddhism like Vajrayāna and Sahajayāna had tremendous influence over certain parts of Odisha. Some of the *siddha*s of these orders like Indrabhūti, Lakṣmīṅkara, Kānhupā, Tantipa, Lui Paa, Saraha Pā and others hailed from this land. Similarly, Nātha Dharma that had already synthesized Tantric Buddhism, Yoga and Śaivism had impacted the culture of the land. Odisha had already established itself as a nerve centre of Tantra. Advaitism of both the forms, Śaṅkaraite and Rāmānujan, had also influenced the religio-philosophical culture of the land.

The depth of the syncretism was so great that Jagannātha (the Vaiṣṇavic deity of the land) was often addressed by the Utkalīya Vaiṣṇavas as the Buddha-Jagannātha. This is something quite unusual in Hindu tradition, i.e. the assimilation of a Hindu deity with Buddha. This assimilation was so deeply ingrained in Odiya culture that the common people of the land never questioned the idea of addressing Jagannātha as Buddha-Jagannātha. Similar peculiarity is observed in the case of pairing of *śūnya* with *Brahman*. This is evident from the fact that the Odiya philosophers, including Bhīmā Bhoi, talk of *Śūnya-Brahman* with self-confidence and without creating any furor in religious and cultural sentiment of the common people. Thus in this case of Mahimā philosophy the possibility of a fusion between diverse philosophical positions cannot be and should not be ignored. I have already quoted some verses from the ancient texts of Nātha Dharma (*Śiśu Veda*, a thirteenth-century text) found in

Odisha that freely use the word *śūnya* with reference to the Highest Reality. We have also noted earlier that some of the keywords of Mahimā metaphysics like *alekha* and *mahimā* were already in vogue in the Odia religio-philosophical tradition much before the arrival of Mahimā Dharma on the scene. In fact, the concepts – *śūnya*, *Brahman* and *pūrṇa* – carried the same implication in this cultural tradition. These words simply imply a non-dualistic philosophy that rests on the ineffability of God.

Despite such extensive use of *śūnya* in the literature of Bhīmā Bhoi it appears confusing that scholars like C.R. Das[33] and even Biśvanātha Bābā,[34] who have written full-fledged books on the philosophical position of Mahimā Dharma, prefer to remain silent on this concept. Their entire analysis of Mahimā philosophy is centred on the concept of *Brahman*. This selective forgetfulness suits their philosophical predilection as they conjectured that the focus on the notion *śūnya* might have stood in the way of putting the ideas of Mahimā Dharma in the straightjacket of Upaniṣadic Advaitism. Biśvanātha Bābā tries to prove that Mahimā Dharma is nothing but Viśuddhādvaitism (unalloyed Advaitisn). Nobody, as such, would disagree with this view. Bhīmā Bhoi's presentation of Mahimā Dharma points to nothing but a pure (*viśuddha*) form of non-dualism. But I want to argue that the use of the word *śūnya* does not come in the way of proving its non-dualistic credentials. From my subsequent discussion about the nature of the *Śūnya-Brahman/Puruṣa* as enunciated by Bhīmā Bhoi my claim would be more than clear. The idea of a pure non-dual principle is so explicit in the works of Mahimā literature that we need not put it in the procrustean bed of Śāstras, Purāṇas and Smṛtis as is attempted by the venerable Avadhūta Biśvanātha Bābā. In the process injustice is done to the unique form of advaitism projected by Bhīmā Bhoi. It is a hard fact that Bhīmā Bhoi's compositions had received the sanction of his Master. Even the worst dissenter of Bhīmā Bhoi

---

[33] C.R. Das, 1959, *Odishara Mahimā Dharma*, Cuttack: Mahimā Dharmalocana Samiti.

[34] Biśvanātha Bābā, *Philosophy of Mahimā Dharma* (tr. S. Das), vol. I, Cuttack: Mahimā Dharmalocana Samiti.

cannot dismiss its veracity. Again, Bhīmā Bhoi could not have used the concept of *śūnya* so extensively without the sanction of Mahimā Svāmī, the founder of the *dharma*. So let us keep an open mind and have a relook at Bhīmā Bhoi's use of the term *śūnya*, especially with reference to the Highest Reality.

The Nature of Śūnya-Brahman/Puruṣa

We have already noted that according to Mahimā Dharma, *Alekha/ Śūnya/Parama-Brahman* is a singular reality who eludes any attempt to delineate it in any form or by any name. But how does one describe such a reality? It transcends all forms that characterize the phenomenal world. Neither the categories of thought nor the forms of speech can envelop it. Its indeterminateness (*nirguṇatva* and *nirviśeṣatva*) evades words. A person's helplessness to explain such a reality is perhaps best expressed in the following lines of Bhīmā Bhoi:

> *The glory and power of the* Brahman *is known to* Brahman *alone.*
> *Who in the three worlds is capable of assessing this infinite*
> Brahman —
> *The one who pervades the universe.*[35]

If at all one has to describe such an entity then it can at best be done through negative predication. In the words of Bhīmā Bhoi:

> *The primordial* Alekha Śūnya-Puruṣa *has no name*
> *Nor colour. He is invisible. How can I know him?*
> *He indescribable, beyond words, beyond Vedas.*[36]

Again,

> O Puruṣa *you are without colour or form*
> *xx xx xx*
> *You have no name*
> *Unnameable you are, indescribable and unseen.*
> *In which form shall I recognize you*

---

[35] *brahmara mahimā brahma jāṇe* । *keva sāmaratha tini bhuvane* । *avyaya brahamku kalibaku achhā he* । – *Bhajanamālā*, II

[36] *Bhajanamālā*, I.22.

You whose greatness is endless?
Unspeakable, beyond the sounds, there is no trace of knowledge
Even as a poet I have no courage to describe you.[37]

According to the Mahimā Dharma, the best way to address this Reality Supreme is possible only through negative epithets such as – unnameable (*anāma/anāmika*), formless (*arūpa*), (without any identifying mark (*avarṇa*)), imperceptible (*adṛśya*), non-describable (*avyakta*), non-qualifiable (*nirguṇa*), taintless (*nirañjana*), beginningless (*anādi*), beyond thought or mind (*amana*) *Śūnya-Brahman*; yet He is the *Prabhu, Parama-Puruṣa* (the Highest Being). This use of negative predication is not something unknown to the Indian philosophical tradition. We cannot simply call it an example of "negative theology"; for in the principle Upaniṣads as well as in Mahāyāna Buddhism there is no theological concept. The entire idea is based on logic pure and simple. When the Highest Reality is ineffable and absolutely non-dual, every attempt to apply a positive predicate or attribute to such a Reality implies its contradictory attribute. So applying a predicate or attribute means to determine it and every determination is limitation – the limitation of non-applicability of its opposite. This way of describing the non-describable is most cryptically stated by *Bṛhadāraṇyaka Upaniṣad* in the form of *neti neti* (not this, not this). But we must remember that this is not something peculiar to Upaniṣads alone. *Prajñāpāramitā Hṛdayagarbha*, the famous Mahāyāna Buddhist text, also uses such an expression, i.e. *neti neti*. Nāgārjuna uses the epithets *niḥsvabhāva* (without any essence) and *niṣprapañca* (without any category of thought), Śaṅkara uses the words *nirguṇa, nirvikalpa, nirviśeṣa*; Vajrayānīs uses *adehī* and *avināśī*. Odia Vaiṣṇavas use such epithets as *anākāra, arūpa* and *avyakta*. Thus we find that this is a common predicament for any philosophical system that defines Reality as beyond the categories of thought and words.

When the philosopher fails to grasp this Absolute in words he even sometimes takes recourse to contradictory predicates. Taking resort to such a method of description is primarily aimed

---

[37] *Bhajanamālā*, translation quoted from Bäumer.

at indicating that a concept of the highest order transcends all contradictions. Such contradictions, as if, dissolve into One. We notice this Mahimā philosophy, as expounded by Bhīmā Bhoi, uses the similar method. For example,

> *He is neither* guru, *nor desciple,*
> *Neither master nor servant.*
> *He iṣ not* brāhmaṇa,
> *Not* cāṇḍāla, *not noble.*
>
> *He is neither woman nor man,*
> *Indeed neither male nor female.*
> *Neither brother nor sister*
> *He is not father, not son.*
>
> *xx xx xx*
>
> *He is neither water nor wind*
> *Neither formless yet has no form*
> *He is neither knowledge nor ignorance*
> *Nor even the conception of Veda.*[38]

He uses a series of such contradictory predicates in the 4th canto of *Brahma-Nirūpaṇa Gītā.*

Bhīmā Bhoi finally conceives such a reality transcending all the contradictions involved in such descriptions as *rūpa* and *arūpa,*[39] *sakāma* and *niṣkāma,*[40] *nirguṇa* and *saguṇa*, and *ādi* and *anādi.*[41] But despite such nebulous descriptions of the Highest Reality, viz. *Śūnya-Brahman*, it is not to be conceived as an abstract metaphysical principle. It is also *Parama-Puruṣa/Īśvara*. Here Mahimā Dharma seems to part ways with the form of Absolutism noticed in the Upaniṣadic and the Advaitic stance of Śaṅkara and his followers. *Alekha Para-Brahman*, no doubt, is a God in the sense that a person

---

38 *Stuti-Cintāmaṇi*, 36th *bolī* (translation quoted from *Verses from the Void* by Bäumer).

39 Ibid.

40 *Bhajanamālā*, I.15.

41 Ibid., II.198.

can worship him, can seek solace in surrendering all thoughts and actions to him and could aspire to realize Him. However, unlike in the orthodox Brāhmanism, God is not symbolized by any idol; nor is He seen as an embodiment of positive yet divine attributes. Again unlike the Brāhmanical religion, God is not to be appeased by any rites, any *mantra*, pilgrimages or religious pomposities.

Monism or Monotheism?

I have stated in the last chapter that Mahimā Dharma in its tenor and spirit is uncompromisingly non-dualistic. It believes that there is but one Reality that admits of no duality. Yet it believes that this reality is not an abstract principle but a God who is an object of devotion. He is one, unique, without form, without any identifying mark, without a name, without qualification, without any conceptual construction, beyond the three *guṇa*s, beyond *kṣara* (non-eternal) and *akṣara* (eternal), beyond *nirguṇa* and *saguṇa*; who at best can be attributed with such non-attributive epithets like *alekha*, *Śūnya-Brahman*, or *nirguṇa Parama Īśvara*. The only epithets used with positive signification are *mahimā* and *Para-Brahman*, both the terms having a non-specific and non-personal connotation. Mahimā temple is called *śūnya mandira* that is marked by the conspicuous absence of a deity. Now what do we call such a form of religion? Should we call it monism? Or else monotheism? We usually believe that monism is a purely metaphysical term, whereas monotheism is a religious concept. It stands for belief in one God. Let us look at how the dictionary defines it. According to *Concise Oxford Dictionary* monotheism means "doctrine or belief that there is one God". On the other hand, monism means "theory or doctrine that denies the existence of a distinction or duality such as that between matter and mind, or God and the world"; and also "the doctrine that only one supreme being exists". According to *Chambers Encyclopedia* (vol. IX, p. 495) monotheism signifies personal and ethical aspects of one God who is also an object of devotion. In this case the relation between the finite and the indefinite is defined in two ways. On the one hand it is a relation of love and on the other the finite individual self is seen as subservient who receives his integration with the religious reality as the gift from God. Nevertheless according to *Encyclopedia of Ethics and Religion* it denotes all those philosophical theories which only recognize a single kind of reality. The distinction between monism and monotheism, though quite thin, is very important to us. Mahimā Dharma definitely believes that there is one God who is called *Alekha Parama-Brahman/Īśvara*. But this is unlike the monotheism of the Semitic religion that believes that there is a distinction between the God and the world; between I and Thou. In this sense we cannot call Mahimā Dharma monotheistic but monistic for its conception of God as the Supreme Reality includes all the diversities of the phenomenal world within its bosom. It admits of no duality at the level of concept as well at the level of ontology between God and the world. In this context M. Hiriyanna's remarks about the distinction between the two concepts are of some relevance to us. He says:

> . . . the monotheistic conception, regarded purely as such is bound to involve duality. What it aims at is only unity of godhead – the reduction of many gods to one who is above and apart from the world which he makes and guides. It regards nature as set over against God and can, therefore, satisfy the longing for unity only in a qualified sense. There is a higher conception of unity, viz. monism which traces the whole of existence to a single source.[42]

One may or may not agree with Hiriyanna regarding his conception of dualism in the form of "nature as set over against God" but this does not come in our way of understanding the core distinction between the basic presuppositions of monism as opposed to monotheism. It has been duly admitted by the scholars that there is no synonym for religion in Indian tradition and *dharma* is but a poor substitute for the word. In fact, in Indian philosophical tradition there is no clear-cut boundary between philosophy and religion since both finally aim at *mokṣa, mukti, niḥśreyasa, apavarga* or *nirvāṇa*, or by whatever name we call it. Keeping this fact in our mind we cannot always sustain a distinction between the philosophical concept of reality and the religious concept of a Supreme Being. So the distinction between

[42] M. Hiriyanna, 1994, *Outlines of Indian Philosophy*, Delhi: Motilal Banarsidass, p. 41.

monism and monotheism amounts to a category of mistake if applied to Indian religio-philosophical tradition. Instead of applying the categories – monism and monotheism – I have taken resort in the word "non-dualism" as in Mahimā Dharma no distinction exists between *Alekha Para-Brahman/Puruṣa* and his creation in the form of the phenomenal world (in the words of Hiriyanna, "nature set over against God"); between individual self (*jīva*) and the universal (*parama*); between the individual body (*piṇḍa*) and the cosmic body (*brahmāṇḍa*); between man and man. Once we understand the true essence of Mahimā conception of God it would be easier for us to understand why this form of religion is to be called non-dualism rather than monotheism. Unlike monotheism of the Semitic variety, in this case God is not seen as the creator who wills that there be a world but he never is a part of it.

What do we call such a conception of God? Are these *sant*s talking of a personal God that forms the very basis of theism? We would be doing injustice to Mahimā Dharma if we understand its conception of God as a personal god. So I entirely agree with S.C. Panigrahi who prefers to label such a reality as "indeterminate subjectivity" or "transcendental subjectivity".[43] This can better explain the Mahimā position on their understanding of *Alekha/Śūnya-Puruṣa/Brahman*. Nowhere in Mahimā literature we do come across the description of a personal god. Mahimā way of looking at God is completely distinct from the usual Hindu conception of God that has dominated Indian religious scene for centuries. Here, albeit God is mentioned, he is not a God in the traditional sense of the term. God is presented as a nameless, formless, indescribable and non-attributable being. So it would be wrong on our part to affiliate this form of faith to any accredited religious systems, including Śaivism, Vaiṣṇavism, Tantric systems like Nāgāntī, Yogāntī or Vedāntī and even Jagannāthism that was the main anchor of religious outlook of the Odia people in general. Bhīmā Bhoi amply enunciates this in following verse:

[43] S.C. Panigrahi, 1998, *Bhīmā Bhoi and Mahimā Dharma*, Bubaneswar: D.S.A. in Philosophy, Utkal University, p. 42.

This is not the dīkṣā *(initiation) of Mahādeva Śiva*[44]
It is much more hard than the path
To pray to alekha mahimā *is not the same as doing* aṣṭāṅga yoga
This is not also the path of Viṣṇu but much profounder.

xx *xx* *xx*

It is not also the path suggested by Nāgāntī or Yogāntī
Rather more stringent than these.
Where the niṣkāma dharma *(of Mahimā) flows*
That alone is Vaikuṇṭha.[45]

We also cannot rely on Veda and Śāstra to have the true knowledge of *Alekha Para-Brahman*. Mahimā conception of Supreme Being, if we go by the account elucidated by Bhīmā Bhoi, transcends even Vedic knowledge. He sometimes describes the four Vedas as the four guards of the temple of *śūnya*. Sometimes he describes the four Vedas as just four books that can be compared to dry leaves.[46]

The so-called wise refer to Veda and Śāstra
But none of them can fathom the true essence of Brahman.
Everybody talks of Brahman,
Seldom they possess the discriminative knowledge of this tattva.[47]

So Bhīmā Bhoi lays the entire emphasis on the concept of *nirveda* that means a path beyond Vedas.[48] Hence, though Mahimā Dharma is not exactly anti-Vedic, yet it does not hold Veda in very high esteem. Thus it displays a form of non-conformism that cannot be taken

---

44 These lines refute Betinna Bäumer's conjecture that "As a theological concept, often combined with *Brahman* or *Puruṣa*, it comes closer to a Hindu (mostly Śaiva) tantric understanding than to the Buddhist concept", p. 44.

45 *Stuti-Cintāmaṇi*, 86th *bolī*.

46 *cāri veda cāri gratha, kita pataṅga je yukta* | *śuṣka patra saṅge lakṣya chādi bhaja ajapāku* | – *Bhajanamālā*, I.29

47 *Brahma-Nirūpaṇa Gītā*, 3rd canto.

48 *śabda upare rahiachhi nirveda* | *veda upare rahichhi nirveda* |
– *Bhajanamālā*, I.32

lightly. Rightly or wrongly, Vedas are held in high esteem in the Indian orthodox tradition; they are claimed to be the fountainhead of all arts and sciences including the so-called Sanātana Dharma. So one may find it really audacious of Bhīmā Bhoi to make the following remarks about those who swear by Vedas:

> *Many may talk of the reality and show the path narrated by Śāstras,*
> *Without ever knowing what the* Brahman *is.*
>
> *xx xx xx*
>
> *They can go as far as Vedas can dictate them not more,*
> *So such people are engaged in unnecessary rites* (karma) *and rituals* (kriyā).[49]

In fact, the path of realizing such a God is so difficult and unusual that Bhīmā Bhoi wonders:

> *When I talked of* śūnya,
> *They fled in fear.*
> *For, it has no shape or sign.*[50]

For such a God can only be realized by direct experience. To realize such a God there is no need for Vedas or higher knowledge (*vidyā*).[51] Here we come across a characteristically distinct trend in which God is described as *śūnya;* and *śūnya* is described as God. In the process the Odiya santic tradition as well as Mahimā Dharma displayed a substantial amount of guts in defying the traditional tenets of Hindu theology. So they do not hesitate to dismiss all that is accepted as sacred and sacrosanct in orthodox Hindu tradition. We had a glimpse of such an unorthodox trend in some of the early writings of the Odiya *sants*. As the years rolled by the Odiya *sants* became bolder and bolder; and in the works of Bhīmā Bhoi we see the complete fructification of this spirit of rebellion. He writes:

---

[49] *Brahma-Nirūpaṇa Gītā*, 16th canto.

[50] Ibid., 3rd canto.

[51] *japa tapa mantre nāhin* । *veda, vidyā, na lāgai*
– *Bhajanamālā* II.191

> One who realizes *Śūnya-Brahman* through true knowledge discards gods and goddesses, all the idols along with the *tantra, mantra* and Vedas.[52]

Illustrating the futility of idol worship Bhīmā Bhoi laments:

> *See what ignorance! Being mere humans,*
> *They relate with the lifeless idols.*
> *Yet we pay no attention to the One*
> *Who created our body and life from* śūnya.
>
> *Without recognizing the Highest Lord*
> *This precious life becomes useless.*
> *In ignorance people worship*
> *Whichever God is more pleasing to their nature.*[53]

But the spirit of breaking free from the chains of orthodoxy is very boldly exhibited when Bhīmā Bhoi goes on to defy even Lord Jagannātha,[54] the ultimate symbol of divinity in Odisha. He very boldly argues:

> If He is the *nātha* (lord) of the *jagat* (the universe) why should he confine himself within the confines of the sanctum of the temple at Purī?[55]

In his famous work *Brahma-Nirūpaṇa Gītā* he goes one step ahead and portrays Jagannātha, the most respected and adored God of Odisha, as the first disciple of Mahimā Svāmī. Till date Mahimāites believe Jagannātha was unhappy with all the corruptions taking place in His name and had permanently left his abode of Śrī Mandira (the temple of Jagannātha) to be with Mahimā Svāmī.

The concept of *Śūnya-Brahman, Alekha Para-Brahman* of the

---

52 *Bhajanamālā*, I.6.

53 *Stuti-Cintāmaṇi*, 95th *bolī* (translation quoted from Bettina Bäumer).

54 Interestingly Bhīmā Bhoi dedicates one whole poem (8th *bolī*) to Lord Jagannātha in his famous treatise *Stuti-Cintāmaṇi*. Maybe he gradually overcame this last trace of the orthodox religious attitude in subsequent works.

55 *Śrutiniṣedha Gītā*, 3rd canto.

Mahimā Dharma is uncharacteristic as a metaphysical theory. Here is a pure absolutistic metaphysics that mingles effortlessly with the religious conception of a godhead.

This illustrates the thin barrier between philosophy and religion mentioned earlier. The same Reality can be viewed as *Brahman* from the metaphysical angle and again as *Īśvara* or *Bhagavān* from a religious angle.[56] However, all said and done certain valid doubts may still linger in our mind. We may agree with Bhīmā Bhoi that the *śūnya* may be taken as the Highest Reality as well as the object of devotion; but how can the ineffable, non-describable and attributeless principle of *śūnya* be related to *saṁsāra* (phenomenal world)? Is the phenomenal world, including the individual souls an apparent manifestation of *Śūnya-Puruṣa* or is it the real manifestation. Interestingly, Bhīmā Bhoi, like his predecessors, viz. the Utkalīya Vaiṣṇavas, views *Śūnya-Puruṣa* as the potential womb of the phenomenal world. So the universe consisting of the conscious and material objects is taken to be the real manifestation of the Highest Being. But such a viewpoint may seem paradoxical, for there is a conceptual gap between the *nirguṇatva* of the Highest Reality and its manifestation as the plurality of names and forms. I intend to examine in the next chapter, how this paradox can be sorted out as far as Mahimā Dharma is concerned.

---

[56] *brahmeti paramātmeti bhagavāna iti sabdyate* ।
– *Śrīmad Bhāgavatam*, I.22

5

Śūnya-Brahman, Jagat and Jīva

WE have noted in the previous chapter that *Śūnya-Brahman* as the self-complete principle includes within the ambit of its conceptualization the transcendence of all dualities. It follows then that there cannot be an iota of distinction between the Supreme Being and the phenomenal world; and consequently between the individual self and Highest Self. No doubt, the phenomenal world is characterized by the pluralities of names and forms; animate and inanimate beings. This definitely comes in the way of holding on to pure non-dualism. There seem to be two options open – either to deny the status of reality to the phenomenal world; or to admit that the absolute is potentially the ground of all diversities. Mahimā Dharma opts for the second conceptual scheme. It conceives Highest Being as the potential ground for the manifestation of the universe with names and forms. Here there is no talk of *māyā* or *avidyā* to explain the non-reality of the universe. Let us examine in this chapter how Mahimā Dharma conceives the entire scheme of emanation/ manifestation of the phenomenal world (*jagat*) from the *śūnya/ alekha/mahimā*; and the relation between the individual self (*jīva*) and the cosmic self, on the one hand, and gross body (*piṇḍa*) and the cosmic body (*brahmāṇḍa*), on the other.

Śūnya-Brahman and Jagat

No metaphysical theory is complete until it successfully explains the relation between the Highest Reality and the phenomenal world. The pluralists and realists do not face any problem. But the problem is enormous in case of the non-dualists. If we take Śaṅkara's Advaitavāda as the model of a rigorous non-dualistic metaphysics then we find that it had to take recourse to some other principles to sort out the issue. Śaṅkara introduces the concept of *māyā* to explain the phenomenal world. *Māyā*, according to Śaṅkara, is the inherent potency of the one and ineffable *Brahman* that acts as the medium of projection of this world of plurality on the non-dual ground of the *Brahman*. Mahimā Dharma does not accept this position. For them the world is the real manifestation of *Śūnya-Brahman*. The *jagat* for them is not unreal and nor is it the product of *māyā*. It is real. *Śūnya-Brahman/Puruṣa / alekha / mahimā* is not an abstract concept. It is the real ground of the phenomenal world. It is the causal matrix.

Interestingly, Mahimā Dharma also draws a distinction between *jagat* and *saṁsāra*. The *saṁsāra* (that is more or less a human creation) is due to the ignorance of *jīva*, the individual self. Due to this ignorance a person thinks that her life is permanent so she craves for ephemeral happiness. Here *māyā* (not in Śaṅkara's sense) seems to be at work. Human beings create their own illusions due to blind obsession for the worldly pleasures. So they are distanced from the Divine Reality. Through the path of moral and spiritual realization an individual can come out of the snare of such wrong mental constructions; and can realize the divinity within. On the other hand, *jagat* is constituted of the world including the animate and inanimate things that emanate from the Divine One. So every speck of it is pervaded by the presence of *Śūnya/Alekha-Brahman*. The true realization comes from the truth that there is no duality between the world and *Parama-Brahman*. This conception comes clearly in the following words of Bhīmā Bhoi:

Wherever I look
– be it moving or the unmoving
– be it insect or bird
You permeate each form
In equal proportion
None is big or small for you.[1]

The extent of *Śūnya-Brahman*'s immanence is as if limitless as is evident from the following verses of Bhīmā Bhoi.

---

[1] *Stuti-Cintāmaṇi*, 15th *bolī*.

You permeate water and earth, fire and air.
You are both, inside and out.
The form of the world,
stays in the formless
As if it has become the essence of all.

Large in large forms, yet small in small,
You are equally within all things,
Living and non-living, in places pure and impure,
Without discrimination – everywhere.

You dwell in the wicked, in the demon and the sinner,
There is nowhere empty of you.
You pervade all beings as their soul,
Bearing the name of Brahman.[2]

The divine presence is so inclusive that even the demonic and wicked are not excluded from this divine spark. This may appear unimaginable for many religio-philosophical systems.

However one may very validly ask – why did *Śūnya-Brahman* manifest himself as the phenomenal world? What compulsion was there on the part of the One to manifest as multiplicity? Bhīmā Bhoi would say that this is due to the will of the Ultimate Reality. Since *Śūnya-Brahman* is beyond our thought and imagination one cannot comprehend the real rationale behind this act. He is univocal about his contention that the creation is due to nothing but the divine will. He calls this will as *icchā vihāra*, some times he names this will as *ājñā*. As the divine presence *Parama-Īśvara* has the divine freedom to manifest himself out of his free will as the universe. This divine freedom to manifest is not held to be an adjunct (*upādhi*) or *guṇa* (attribute) of the Supreme Reality. This rather constitutes the essence of His Being. At the same time when manifesting itself it does not remain outside of the phenomenal world as a mere spectator but permeates everywhere and in every activity; yet He remains beyond its self-manifestation as the universe, as a transcendental

[2] *Stuti-Cintāmaṇi*, 47th *bolīs* 3-6.

being. Its immanence does not rob of the transcendence of the Supreme Reality. He makes things more clear when he says, "there can be none greater than *mahimā*, as it pervades the three worlds".[3] The Supreme Reality manifests itself in two forms – as the Transcendental Being; and also as the Universal Being. In its capacity as the Universal Being *Śūnya-Brahman* permeates and pervades the entire universe as the Immanent Reality. Here one may be reminded of the Upaniṣadic declaration:

He (the supreme soul) desired,
Let me be many, let me be born.[4]

But at this stage another ticklish issue seems to crop up. If this universe is the real manifestation of *Śūnya-Puruṣa*, as indicated by the above verses then obviously a paradox arises. How could an indeterminate, non-qualitative and absolutely non-dual principle manifest itself as plurality of forms and names? Either we accept that the Reality is *saguṇa* (qualitative), hence the manifestation as real (*pariṇāma*); or else, we view the Highest Reality as *nirguṇa* (non-qualitative) and the manifestation as apparent (*vivartta*). In any case, indeterminateness of the Highest Reality and the determinateness of the phenomenal world (*jagat*) may not go together. A look into the *āstika* tradition shows that, excepting Advaita Vedānta, in most of the cases, the Highest Reality is taken as *saguṇa*, therefore they face no problem in explaining the world as the real manifestation of the Highest Reality. But the problem continues to be inexplicable for any non-dualist who insists on the non-attributiveness (*nirguṇatva*) and ineffability of the Highest Reality. However, it will not be out of context to point out how another non-dualist system tries to solve the paradox. This was done by Yogācāra Buddhism with the help of the concept of *abhūta-parikalpa*. The idea was further developed by the Vajrayānīs.

> The word *abhūta-parikalpa* literally means – that which is devoid of all misconceptions or false mental constructions, i.e. the substratum where there is the *mere possibility of subjectivity and*

---

[3] *Brahma-Nirūpaṇa Gītā*, 10th canto.

[4] *Taittirīya Upaniṣad*, 2.6.1.

objectivity – but in which the duality has no reality.[5]

In simpler terms, it implies that though the empirical world is a creation of false mental constructions, it is not absolutely chimeral, because the Highest Reality holds the possibility of subjective–objective distinction. Therefore, it can be taken to be the potential womb of all creations. The concept of creation is impossible without assuming the distinction between the subject and the object. According to S.B. Dasgupta the Vajrayāna conception of the ineffable God is an offshoot of the *yogācārī* theory of *abhūta-parikalpa*.[6] So we find Anaṅgavajra, a *siddha* of the Vajrayānic order professing that it is better to take the world as real than to think everything as unreal. Unless it is conceived so, the very idea of *nirvāṇa* will lose its significance.[7] This is what is meant when Anaṅgavajra describes the Highest Reality as *Śūnyatā-garbha* (womb).[8] Like the Vajrayānī notion of *Śūnyata-garbha,* the *sant*s of Odisha, including Bhīmā Bhoi, present *Śūnya-Puruṣa/Brahman* as the potential womb of the cosmos.[9] While presenting the cosmological account of the phenomenal world Bhīmā Bhoi often uses the word *mahimā-garbha*. Describing the unlimited potency of *mahimā-garbha* Bhīmā Bhoi says:

> *From its womb arises the unlimited,*
> *This is so expansive that it is beyond all conception.*
> *Fifty-six crore animate beings arise from* mahimā
> *Also the thirty-three crore gods and goddesses owe their origin to it.*[10]

---

[5] Dasgupta, *Introduction to Tantric Buddhism*, p. 22.

[6] Ibid., pp. 22-28.

[7] *Prajñopāya Viniścaya Siddhi*, quoted in Dasgupta, p. 36.

[8] Ibid., p. 32.

[9] Hereby I do not want to claim that Mahimā conception of the cosmogony is straightaway lifted from Buddhism. The contradiction of admitting the reality of the world with plurality of names and forms continues to be a problem for any system of thought that takes recourse to non-dualism.

[10] *Brahma-Nirūpaṇa Gītā*, 7th canto.

> Everything arises from *mahimā-garbha*, including day and night, sun and moon, vice and virtue, good and bad, life and death, the process continues incessantly, fifty-six crore living beings.[11]

Interestingly, even the traditional Hindu gods and goddesses are also a part of the manifestation of the *mahimā/alekha*.

Sometimes Bhīmā Bhoi offers a very metaphorical imagery of *Śūnya-Brahman*:

> *His head is the dense void,*[12] *his belly is the earth*
> *The underworld his feet. From the pores of his skin*
> *Emerge clusters and clusters of worlds,*
> *High mountains rise and set.*[13]

So Mahimā Dharma solves the problem of the many from the one with the help of the notion of *Śūnya-Brahman* as the potential ground of all diversities.

Once a philosophical system admits the reality of the phenomenal world there seems to be a compulsion on its part to explain the process of evolution. Therefore the Mahimā Dharma also takes a lot of interest in cosmogony. It is the natural outcome of their philosophical stance. However, in their case the task is daunting, as they have taken the ineffable *śūnya* as the Highest Reality. As per Mahimā account:

> *Then there was nothing*
> *Only* śūnya *and* mahāśūnya
> *Darkness enveloping all*
> *Neither was there the sun and the moon*
> *Nor nine lakh of stars and planets.*
> *Then no distinction between the day and the night*
> *For they are his own creation.*
> *At that point of time there were*

---

11 *Brahma-Nirūpaṇa Gītā*, 7th canto.

12 Absolute void.

13 *Stuti-Cintāmaṇi*, 13th *bolī*. The verse reminds us of the Puruṣa-Sūkta of *Ṛgveda*.

No heaven and hell,
No Brahmā, Viṣṇu or Śiva.

xx xx xx

From the abode of soundless anāma śakti
Took birth the śūnya.
From śūnya *took shape the colours.*
Then arose fire and ether.

xx xx xx

From the nameless arose the three guṇas
Sattva, rajas *and* tamas.

xx xx xx

From the nameless formless
Emerged the sun and the moon
And the pañcabhūtas *(five gross elements).*[14]

Thus, Bhīmā Bhoi conceives the gradual creation from the inexplicable, the nameless and the formless One. We know that the theory of creation is one of the important aspects of philosophical speculation in India. The mysterious universe with all its assorted manifestations in the form of astral, living and non-living entities has made the philosophers curious about the why and how of the creation of the universe. This curiosity is reflected right from the Nāsadīya-Sūkta of *R̥gveda* to Sāṁkhya and then to varied cosmogonical accounts provided in different religio-philosophical systems. But the basic question that is likely to haunt us is – If the reality is formless how can it give rise to the universe characterized by names and forms? Bhīmā Bhoi has perhaps a very convincing explanation for this. He says, the reality being an all-enveloping principle the contradiction between "form" and "formless" does not hold any significance since it transcends all the contradictory appellations and is beyond conceptual categorization.

From the form to formless,

---

[14] *Stuti-Cintāmaṇi*, 78th *bolī.*

From the formless to form
Hari is present everywhere.[15]

Again,

Arūpa *is within* rūpa *as* Brahma svarūpa.[16]

We come across similar explanations in the philosophy of the *sant* predecessors of Bhīmā Bhoi. Acyutānanda, for example, explains:

All these forms are the creations
Of the formless
All manifestations of forms will
Ultimately realize in the formless.
Thus one ought to be able to look at the two as one.
Only by looking at the seemingly opposite
With an attitude of equanimity,
Can one realize the whole range of truth?[17]

Śūnya-Brahman and Jīvātman

Regarding the question of the relationship between *jīva* (individual self) and *Brahman*, which is often addressed as *parama*, Mahimā Dharma strictly adheres to their non-dualistic stand. Thus *jīva* and *Brahman* are viewed as one and identical. This theory can be placed in sharp contrast to the general Vaiṣṇavic position. The Vaiṣṇava ontological position is primarily dualistic. Rāmānuja, one of the greatest exponents of Vaiṣṇavism, despite his monistic attitude, could not think of an unalloyed identity between *jīvātman* and *paramātman*. He rather argues that the individual soul cannot lose its identity, for such a loss of identity would be tantamount to the destruction of the self. Rāmānuja, it seems, was bound by a metaphysical compulsion to accommodate the *bhakti* theory. So he argues that if the *jīva*'s individuality is lost then who will indulge in devotion. The subsequent Vedāntin Vaiṣṇavas were more vociferous about the continuation of

---

15 *Stuti-Cintāmaṇi*, 17th *bolī*.

16 *Bhajanamālā*, I.57.

17 Acyutānanda Dāsa, *Tattvabodhini*.

individuality of the *jīva* even in the state of highest self-realization. They are very unambiguous in their claim that a liberated soul only attains the nature of God, never the identity of God.[18]

I have stated earlier that the Utkalīya Vaiṣṇavas not only deviated from the general Vaiṣṇavic ideology but resorted to a pure non-dualism by ascribing non-attributiveness (*nirguṇatva*) and indescribability (*śūnyatva*) to the Reality Supreme. So they adhered to the theory of total identity of *jīvātman* and *paramātman*. We notice the continuation of the same trend in Mahimā Dharma. In Mahimā parlance there is no duality between *jīva* and *parama*. *Mukti* or ultimate realization for human self refers to the realization of this identity. So Bhīmā Bhoi declares:

> Brahman *is within the* jīva.
> *As the water is within the kernel of coconut,*
> *Similarly the* Brahman *is within your body.*
>
> *xx xx xx*
>
> *The so-called* jñānī *seeks for it outside,*
> *Without ever realizing that Brahman is within.*[19]

Again,

> *Jīva is relentlessly pining for the parama.*
> *With true realization*
> *you find both of them at the same space.*[20]

At first sight, this theory of identity appears very similar to the Advaitic position. But a deeper look at the Mahimā position reveals the originality of its approach. First, Śaṅkara's *jīva–Brahman* identity theory is primarily centred on his conception *jñāna* as the mode of self-realization. *Bhakti* has no place in his metaphysical scheme. But unlike the Advaita Vedāntins the Odisha *sant* tradition, in general,

---

[18] *nāpi nirastavidayasya svarūpaikya sambhavaḥ* ।
— Rāmānuja, *Śrī-Bhāṣya*, I.1.1

[19] *Brahma-Nirūpaṇa Gītā*, VI.

[20] Ibid., 18.

and Mahimā Dharma, in particular, place *jīva–parama* identity in the background of a *bhakti* theory. At the same time one may note a wonderful amalgamation of *bhakti* and *jñāna* in the philosophy of Mahimā Dharma. Thus *bhakti* accentuated by *jñāna* is seen as the path charted out for the realization of the *parama* in the *jīva*. So their task and approach are different from the Advaitavāda. Second, what makes the Mahimā theory of *jīva–parama* identity radically distinct from the Advaita position is its adherence to the *piṇḍa–brahmāṇḍa* identity theory. We may find a glimpse of the idea in the verse quoted above that implies "*Brahman* is within your body". The proclaimed identity between *jīva* and *parama* is used by Mahimā Dharma as a step to facilitate the view that there could be no distinction between *piṇḍa* (gross individual body) and *brahmāṇḍa* (cosmic body). So they hold that the Supreme Consciousness is very much there in the human body itself; and is realizable in this body alone. Bhīmā Bhoi often uses the word *ghaṭa* (pot) to refer to the *piṇḍa* (the individual body) and pleads to make it the means of self-realization.[21] *Jīvātman* and *paramātman* are not distinct. Both of them can be realized in the same body. The identification of *ātman* and *Brahman* is not a novel concept but rarely do we come across such a description of the embodied universal consciousness which stands for *paramātman*.

The Body as the Seat of Divinity

Since Mahimā Dharma subscribes to the theory of *piṇḍa–brahmāṇḍa* identity, for them body itself is the seat of divinity. Human body is not profane or polluted as it has been assumed in our Sanātana Dharma, in general. Though Śaṅkarācārya compares the body with the temple (*deha devālaya prokto*), this idea was not further developed in our orthodox philosophical tradition. With the advent of the Purāṇic age and with the introduction of the concept of *pūjā*, more and more emphasis was laid on the purificatory rites of the body, ritual bathing and mortification of the body. This theory of

---

[21] *bāhyare khojile keve nahi mile* ।
ghaṭa bhedāntare bheṭa pāi ॥ – *Bhajanamālā*, II.192

piṇḍa–brahmāṇḍa identity, of course, as a theory is not an original Mahimāite concept. This theory is adopted by many post-Classical systems of thought influenced by Nātha Dharma and the Buddhist school of Sahajayāna, an offshoot of Tantric Buddhism. In fact, Lakṣmīṅkara, one of the eminent *siddha*s of Sahajayāna Buddhism (she incidentally was the sister of Indrabhūti, the *siddha* of Vajrayāna and the king of Odisha), was one of the first proponents of this theory of *kāya sādhanā*. She proclaimed that we must offer worship to our body, because God is present not in the idols but within one's own body.

Similarly, Saraha Pā, another *siddha* of this order, who is believed to have spent a considerable time of his life in Odisha, says:

> Scholars explain many scriptures, but fail to know that Buddha resides in the body.[22]

Again he writes:

> Someone bodiless is hiding in the body – he who knows him there (within the body) is liberated.[23]

In this context the following line of Bhīmā Bhoi is really noteworthy:

> Though not ordinarily visible, the bodyless is hiding within one's own body.[24]

The emphasis on the practical aspect of *yoga* along with an uncompromising revolt against all formalities and orthodoxy in religion resulted in laying stress on the human body (*piṇḍa*) as a microcosm of the universe (*brahmāṇḍa*). This feature predominates in all the forms of Tantra in general. It was, however, Nātha Dharma which provided a systematic account of the idea of body as the seat of divinity with the theory of *piṇḍa–brahmāṇḍa* identity. The theory is

---

[22] *Dohākosa of Sarahapa*, quoted in N.K. Sahu, Bhubaneswar: Utkal University Press, 1958, p. 139.

[23] *Dohākośa of Sarahapa*, quoted in Dasgupta, *Obscure Religious Cults*, p. 90.

[24] *adehi dehe acchi, se je na diśuchhi* ।
– *Bhajanamālā*, II.218

based on the presupposition that the body (*piṇḍa*) is the medium of the experience of the cosmic self (*brahmāṇḍa*). I have already stated that both Sahajayāna and Nātha Dharma had immense influence on the cultural milieu of Odisha. By thirteenth century CE many works of Nātha Dharma composed in archaic Odia were popular in Odisha. By fifteenth century CE Sāralā Dāsa, the famous Odia *sant*, incorporated this idea in his regional version of *Mahābhārata*. The theory continued to form an important aspect of the Utkalīya Vaiṣṇavism of the Pañcasakhā and their followers. This is evident from the following verse of Acyutānanda Dāsa:

Within your body there is infinite space
The cosmos itself is within your body.
The person who has not penetrated the body,
(Has not understood the power of the body)
His wisdom is of no avail.
Those who do not see me within the body,
How can they know me?[25]

We notice a resurrection of this theory of the divinity of the body in Mahimā philosophy as projected by Bhīmā Bhoi. He categorically says:

Without taking cognizance of the Brahman *within one's own body,*
People unnecessarily search for it outside.
Thinking the idols to be the real One,
They remain contended.
The Lord of the universe is within your body,
Why waste time in worshipping the idol?[26]

Elaborating further on this idea he says:

May you journey into your body
And create therein
The vast universe.

---

[25] Acyutānanda Dāsa, *Caurāsī Yantra.*

[26] *Śrutiniṣedha Gītā.*

May you perform the rites of yoga
And roam around within your body.
May you locate
within your body
holy pilgrimages,
of the outside world.
None so foolish
as a yogī *who wanders*
from place to place on earth.[27]

Prior to Bhīmā Bhoi, three centuries back, the famous Odiya Sant Balarāma Dāsa in his work *Brahmāṇḍa Bhūgola* started the trend of comparing the body with the temple of Lord Jagannātha. His contemporaries and followers also compared different parts of the body to different pilgrim centres. A similar view is expressed by another eminent *sant*, Caitanya Dāsa. He says that *ātman* and *Brahman* are within our body as if chained by the bond of physical existence. Once the *ātman* leaves this body it can have eternal rest in the *śūnya*.[28]

Bhīmā Bhoi not only reiterates this wonderful idea in the last part of the nineteenth century, he also argues that human birth is a rare gift of the Almighty.[29] This idea of the rarity of birth in human form is reiterated again and again so that human beings do not while away time in insignificant chores of life. There is a sense of urgency in Bhīmā Bhoi's tone to realize the divinity within the body in this birth itself – as neither the body, nor the *prāṇa*, nor time – nothing is permanent. "Once this body dies where is the question of rebirth? Even if there is rebirth how do you know when it will happen?"[30] So it

27 *Stuti-Cintāmaṇi*, 84th *bolī* (translation quoted from Siddhartha Satpathy, 2006); Bhīmā Bhoi*: Prayers and Reflections*, Bhubaneswar: Rupantar.

28 Caitanya Dāsa, *Nirguṇa Māhātmya*, XII.

29 *durlabha janama manuṣya sarīra saṁsāre kāla sara* ।
– *Stuti-Cintāmaṇi*, 39th *bolī*

30 *e deha chādile janma kahin* । *kebe janma heba hetu nāhin* ।
– *Bhajanamālā* II.13

is better to use your body for the *siddhi* by following the path of *jñāna*.

Layers of Śūnya

One of the most interesting dimensions of the *śūnya*-centric metaphysics is the stratification of *śūnya* in multiple layers. Both Sahajayāna Buddhism and non-dualist Śaivism talk of several stages of the experience of *śūnya*. *Svacchanda Tantra*, a text of Kashmir Śaivism, for example, talks of seven stages of *śūnya* through which a *yogī* has to pass in the process of his spiritual ascent. Nāgārjunapāda, the famous Buddhist tantric (who had consequential influence on Odisha culture), in his treatise *Pañcakarma*, offers a hierarchical scheme of *śūnya*, viz. *śūnya, atiśūnya, mahāśūnya* and *sarvaśūnya*.[31] Interestingly, the Odia *sant*s also follow this trend in classifying *śūnya*. Acyutānanda Dāsa talks of three grades of *śūnya*, viz. *śūnya, mahāśūnya* and *jyoti*, whereas, Yaśovanta Dāsa talks of four, viz. *śūnya, jyotirśūnya, mahāśūnya* and *cetanā*.[32] Some even stratify seventy-two layers of *śūnya*. As such this classification of *śūnya* does not seem to add any new depth to their theory of *Śūnya-Puruṣa*, but it may be connected with their theory of yogic *sādhanā*. Most probably they were following a tradition already set by the *siddha*s of Vajrayāna and Sahajayāna Buddhism. We notice that though Bhīmā Bhoi appears on the scene almost after three centuries he follows this pattern of talking of the layers of *śūnya*. For him *śūnya* has three layers. The first *śūnya* is *sthūla śūnya*; this is the abode of *nirākāra*. The second *śūnya* is the abode of Mahimā Gosain. The final *śūnya* is the abode of the *alekha*.[33] Like the other *sant*s of this land he believes that the experience of the highest level of *śūnya* is self-luminous light (*jyoti*). This view is of specific interest to us. Here the influence of this Buddhist *siddha*s seems to be more pronounced. So we find Jagannātha Dāsa describing *Brahman* as *śūnya jyoti*[34] whereas Acyutānanda Dāsa describes the intuitive

---

31 Referred in Dasgupta, p. 43 n, also pp. 43-46.

32 Acyutānanda Dāsa, *Śūnya Saṁhitā Causaṭhī Ṭīkā*.

33 *Brahma-Nirūpaṇa Gītā*, XIII.

34 Jagannātha Dāsa, *Tuḷa Bhiṇā*.

experience of this effulgent light as the experience of God Himself.[35] Interestingly, *Siddha-Siddhānta-Paddhati*, a work of the Nātha cult also projects the *saccidānanda Brahman* as the *jyoti*, i.e. *svajyoti satyamekam jayati tava padaṁ sacchidānandamūrte*.[36] It is interesting to note that the Mahimā-panthīs do not worship any God but look sun-wards and chant the name of *alekha*. Here sun *stands* for the same principle of *jyoti* or the effulgent light. This divine experience is thus achievable with the phenomenal body here and now. This also makes it evident that the Odia *sant*s including Bhīmā Bhoi, believed in *jīvanmukti*, not in *videhamukti*.

---

[35] *śūnyaśūnya mahāśūnya madhye jyoti* ।
tat jyoti bhagavāna svayam ।
– Quoted in K. Kara, 1989, *Ascarya Caracaya*, Bhubaneswar: Orissa Sahitya Akademi, p. 195

[36] *Siddha-Siddhānta-Paddhati*, quoted in K. Kara, p. 196.

6

Man and God

WE have noted in the previous chapter that in Bhīmā Bhoi's estimation God, viz. *Śūnya-Puruṣa/Śūnya-Brahman,* permeates every individual souls be he a saint or be he a wicked person or a demon. The divinity is within every conscious body and soul. This divine spark needs an outlet. So it is natural for man to overcome the bondage of his finitude and to be in the quest for the infinite and divine. This thrust comes from within. This, in the true sense of the term, is the very basis of religion. No amount of prescriptions from outside, no amount of lure for a berth in the heaven can move a true seeker of the divine truth. There are various ways suggested in the Indian tradition for the achievement of the goal. Some insist on the path of devotion (*bhakti*), pure and simple, some others again lay emphasis on true intuitive knowledge (*jñāna*). The history of Indian religious theories reveals that the path of *jñāna* is always given a backseat and *bhakti* holds its sway as far as the conception of self-realization/*mukti*/*mokṣa* is concerned. Again there is no unanimity of opinion as far the scope and the limit of the notion of *bhakti* is concerned. Mahimā Dharma very explicitly advocates *bhakti* as the mode that fulfils a man's yearning for self-realization. At the same time it sees no dichotomy between the path of *jñāna* and the path of *bhakti*. At a first look the Mahimā attitude to the entire issue seems to be riddled with confusions.

We have observed that Mahimā Dharma does not conform to the norms of what is ordinarily known as religious forms of belief in Hinduism. First and foremost, there is no conception of God with a form or figure. It subscribes to no major accredited systems of Hindu belief like Vaiṣṇavism, Śaivism and Śāktism. The Mahimā-panthīs are non-dualists though not exactly monotheists. Their conception of God is in a sense different from other forms of monotheism. *Śūnya-Puruṣa,* though an object of devotion, continues to be formless. Once the Highest Reality is conceived as of the nature of *śūnya* and indescribable principle rather than an entity embodied in a form, there is bound to be a difference in the implications of the very notion of *bhakti*. The problem seems to be more perplexing when *bhakti* is linked to *jñāna*. My basic job in this chapter is untying these knoty issues. But before I explicate the concept of *bhakti* of Mahimā Dharma I deem it proper to examine in brief two important forms of *bhakti* theory – *saguṇa* and *nirguṇa*. This may be helpful for us in making a proper assessment of the ingenuity of the Mahimā theory of *jñāna-bhakti*.

Bhakti: The Two Dimensions

If we look at the dynamics of the word *bhakti,* we may note that it is neither necessarily connected with the notion of a personal god nor with the emotional mode of devotion. Unfortunately there is a trend among the modern scholars and Indologists to avoid a detailed analysis of the multiple nuances associated with the varied forms of *bhakti* theories that flourished in this land. First, most often *bhakti* is understood in terms of emotion/emotinal state (*bhāva*), something very opposed to self-analytical and intuitive method of realizing the highest object of devotion. Second, the notion of a personal god is always dragged in. Many scholars seem to resist any attempt to explore the possibility of an alternative explication of the term. Here I take G.C. Pande's following lines as a case in point. In the proccedings of a seminar, entitled *Bhakti*, published as late as 2000 he observes:

> Religion is possible without belief in a personal god. There may be a religion without belief in a personal god, but it cannot be called atheism. It is also theism: it is religion. But *bhakti* without faith, without belief in a personal god is not possible.[1]

---

[1] Daya Krishna et al. (eds.), 2000, *Bhakti: A Contemporary Discussion*, New Delhi: ICPR, p. 47.

It is clear that Pande tries to draw a line between religion and *bhakti*. We whole-heartedly admit that the two concepts are distinct. So when he talks of a religion without a god perhaps he has in mind the original Buddhism as a religion that did not subscribe to the notion of a personal god. But he seems to forget that if religion is possible without God so also is *bhakti*. There are many *bhakti* schools that do not reconcile with the conception of a personal deity. Now that we have already explicated the Mahimā theory we can safely claim there is at least one such *bhakti* school[2] that does not subscribe to the concept of a personal god.

A close look at the evolution and development of *bhakti* as a mode of self-realization/God-realization reveals that there are two models available that may be labelled as *saguṇa-bhakti* and *nirguṇa-bhakti*. The Āḷvārs and the southern *ācārya*s like Rāmānuja, Vallabha, Madhva and Nimbārka and also Gauḍīya Vaiṣṇavism of Śrī Caitanya followed the *saguṇa* path. They believed in a personal god endowed with divine qualities; hence describable in nature. On the other hand, thinkers like Kabīr, Dādū, Rajjab and the Odia *sant*s including the Mahimā-panthīs prefer to follow the path of *nirguṇa-bhakti*. For them *bhakti* does not necessarily mean devotion to a personal god, who could be described in terms of specific positive attributes. God for them is non-qualifiable; hence ineffable.

The other benchmark of *saguṇa-bhakti* model is the emphasis laid on the element of love. It is well known that the Vaiṣṇava *ācārya*s of the south India introduced the element *bhakti* in their interpretation of the philosophy of Vedānta. But love as a basic component of *bhakti* gets foothold with Vallabha's introduction of a dichotomy between the *puṣṭi mārga* and *maryādā mārga*. The *puṣṭi mārga* is accorded superiority on the ground that it is based on an intense attachment for *Īśvara* without a trace of dependence on *jñāna*. *Maryādā mārga*, on

[2] Even the *nirguṇa* philosophers like Kabīr and Rajjab did not believe in a personal god. Did not Kabīr make specifically clear that whenever he refers to Rāma, he is not referring to a personal god, viz. an incarnation of Viṣṇu? Rāma is a symbol of the Reality Supreme. Yet Kabīr preached the importance of *bhakti* as a part of self-realization.

the other hand, is the path followed by the *yogī*s who rely on *jñāna* as one of the important components of the path to self-realization.

Not only does *saguṇa-bhakti mārga* insist on a personal god as one of its basic presupposition, it also presupposes that God has a form and name with infinite divine attributes (*saguṇa*). Unless God is conceived without attributes *bhakti* cannot be explained in terms of emotional attachment. Love implies an object of love who could be adored with all its lovable attributes. Hence they follow Śāṇḍilya's definition of *bhakti* as intense emotional attachment to God (*paramānuraktinirīśvare*).

Finally, the *saguṇa* mode of *bhakti* under no circumstances would admit of the non-difference between *paramātman* and *jīvātman*. A line of distinction, however thin, is maintained between the *paramātman* and *jīvātman* (under no circumstances the gap could be overcome). A *bhakta* does not seek identity (*ekātmatā*) with God.[3] He/She aims at service of God and actions for his delight. It cannot be a relationship of *tādātmya* (identity).

Nirguṇa-bhakti model on the other hand is not centred on the idea of a personal god. According to the advocates of this theory God is beyond all conceptualizations and categories of thought. So no qualities can be ascribed to Him; hence He is *nirguṇa*. God is nameless and formless. Though love is highlighted as a qualification of a seeker, *bhakti* is not just an emotional state. Rather the realization of the identity between the *jīvātman* and *paramātman* forms the basic foundation of the path of *nirguṇa upasanā*. So in this case *jñāna* or the realization of *paramātman* in *ātman* plays a major role. This model comes closest to Śaṅkarācārya's definition of *bhakti* as investigation into one's own self (*sva-svarūpānusandhāna*).

The major philosophical trend of Odisha during the medieval period was tilted more towards *nirguṇa-bhakti* rather than *saguṇa-*

---

[3] A popular line in Vaiṣṇava literature explains beautifully the logic behind their claim of non-identity between the devotee and the object of devotion. "I want to eat sugar, not be sugar myself" (*chini hote chaina ami chini khete chai*).

bhakti. This had a lot to do with their conception of God as formless, indescribable *Śūnya-Puruṣa/Brahman*. Such a God, though He can be an object of *bhakti*, could only be realized through the direct knowledge of the identity between the individual self (*jīva*) and God (*parama*). Here *bhakti* has a new connotation – it is *bhakti* accentuated by *jñāna*.

Jñāna and Bhakti: The New Perspective

One may note that the conception of *jñāna-bhakti* or *bhakti* accentuated by *jñāna* propagated by the Utkalīya Vaiṣṇavas is conceptually independent of other Vaiṣṇavic forms of *bhakti*. To make a proper assessment of the conception of *jñāna-bhakti* let me offer succinct account of the theory of the Utkalīya Vaiṣṇavism. According to these thinkers *bhakti* and *jñāna* should not be seen as antithetical; rather *bhakti* and *jñāna* co-mingle at certain point of a man's spiritual journey. In Acyutānanda's words:

> *By penetrating* jñāna *one gets* bhakti,
> *And by penetrating* bhakti *one gets* jñāna.[4]

But if we probe deeper into the theory of these *sant*s it becomes clear that *jñāna* is given a priority. Here *jñāna* means self-knowledge (*ātma-jñāna*), not the scriptural knowledge, i.e. *vidyā*.[5] With this emphasis on *ātma-jñāna*, *bhakti* is defined as that experience which emerges from the knowledge of non-duality between *jīva* and *Īśvara*. In other words it is a form of devotion towards the Ultimate Reality in which case the bliss of *bhakti* (devotion) is realizable once the identity between *jīvātman* and *paramātman* is experienced. This is called *brahmānubhūti*. Summerizing their stand on the issue Dvārakā Dāsa, a seventeenth-century *sant*, says:

> There are innumerable paths suggested by different persons. Men fail to realize that there is but one *Brahman*. All these paths are of no avail without realizing the *Brahman* in *ātman*.[6]

---

[4] Acyutānanda Dāsa, *Gurubhakti Gītā*, III.50.

[5] Acyutānanda Dāsa, *Śabda-Brahma Saṁhitā*, I.

[6] Dvārakā Dāsa, *Trayodasa Bhāgavata*, VII.

It may be a difficult path, but one has a scope to go step by step.

The Mahimā Concept of Jñāna-Bhakti

I have all along argued that the Mahimā philosophy has a close connection with the general philosophical inclination of the medieval *sant* tradition that grew in Odisha right from fifteenth century onwards. In general Bhīmā Bhoi seems to share a similar view on the issue. But the presentation of his theory is bolder and has more dimensions. One can also easily discern certain uniqueness in the formulation of the theory. No doubt, like the medieval *sant*s he forges a synthesis between *jñāna* and *bhakti*; at the same time warning that these two terms should not be taken at their facevalue:

> *Everybody speaks of* jñāna
> *But nobody realizes how difficult the path is*
> *Everybody speaks of* bhakti
> *But that does not allow them to be one with the* Brahman.[7]

So we have to take a deep look at the implications of both the terms, i.e. *jñāna* and *bhakti*. We have already noted in the previous chapter that according to Bhīmā Bhoi, the Reality Supreme, viz. *Śūnya-Brahman* is present within every human form (be he a good or a demonic person) as *ātman*. So the infinite dwells in every finite being. One can realize the divinity within by true knowledge. *Jñāna-mārga* does not stand for the worship of God as an object different from the self. So he makes it clear that *jñāna* or knowledge is not to be confused with the intellect or the knowledge of the Śāstras and Vedas. There is a distinction between the *jñāna* and *buddhi-jñāna* – the intellectual knowledge. He warns that *buddhi-jñāna* or the knowledge of Śāstras cannot take us very far in our quest for self-realization. What is needed is (what he calls as *sad-jñāna*) the spiritual knowledge or true intuitive knowledge. This type of knowledge alone can lead to the knowledge of the unknown, and experience the *śūnya svarūpa* (essence). Since true knowledge is not a matter of academic deliberation there is no scope here for dialectics or logic. So he makes it clear:

---

[7] *Brahma-Nirūpaṇa Gītā*, XIV.

Those who do not know claim to know the Brahman
Such false claims make them more confused.
Those who know the Brahman *keep it to themselves*
Without any argument or false claim.
He is indivisible
Do not split him through logic.[8]

Again, *jñāna* should be seen as distinct from *kalpanā*. Here *kalpanā* does not mean imagination but the empirical knowledge. One has to transcend the empirical level of knowledge to attain true *jñāna*. The more one progresses in the path of knowledge the more one realizes the limitations of the human intellect. So true *jñāna* can ultimately be described as *ātmopāsanā* (worship of God within the self). Such *sad-jñāna* alone can help man to come out of the vortex of birth–death cycle.

But, how does one achieve such a state of *sad-jñāna*? Bhīmā Bhoi's answer again is quite straightforward:

Make your body the seat of knowledge
Then only would you realize that
The *alekha* formless is in every being.[9]

The above-mentioned verse makes it clear that the path of *jñāna* consists in the realization of the absolute within one's own self and within one's own body. One may note that the emphasis on body at some level has also deep connection with the yogic method of *kāyā sādhanā*. This is why Bhīmā Bhoi often talks of *a-mana sādhanā*. *Mana* is the mind which is constantly subject to fanciful and wandering thought. Controlling this trend of mind and concentrating on fancy-free mindfulness is called *a-mana sādhanā*. He also very often uses such tantric-yogic terms as *sahasrāra*, etc. Yet he realizes that the path of true knowledge is quite arduous, so he takes recourse to the theory of *bhakti* to make the unachievable achievable. Regarding the question – how such difficult path could be treaded? – his answer is simple. This can only be possible through *bhakti*. Thus he connects

---

[8] *Stuti-Cintāmaṇi*, 49th *bolī*.

[9] *Bhajanamālā*, I.38.

jñāna and *bhakti* by the same bond of spiritual knowledge. As Bhīmā Bhoi says:

> The secrets of *jñāna* are unheard and unspeakble,
> Can you achieve this without *bhakti*?[10]

Here *bhakti*, however, is not seen as anything truly distinct from the *jñāna*. Both are so complementary that one is likely to notice no line of demarcation. We have already noted that Mahimā Dharma firmly adheres to faith in the absoluteness of the self and recognizes no other reality than *ātman*. So a *jñānī* is a *bhakta* and a *bhakta* is a *jñānī*. Such a person treats the high and the low, the animate and the inanimate alike because of his realization that different selves housed in different bodies are in fact of the same nature. So he sees everyone in himself; and himself in everyone. A *bhakta* with this knowledge has to expand his mind and soul to all that exists in the world. So Bhīmā Bhoi clearly points out that a *jñānī*:

> *Sees everything as his own* ātman,
> *He claims everybody to be his own*
> *For he belongs to everybody.*[11]

A realized soul therefore "finds duality nowhere, neither between pain and happiness nor between man and man". Further he points out:

> *Direct your mind to the*
> *Self-illumined* śūnya
>
> *xx xx xx*
>
> *If you have right experience*
> *You can have a glimpse of the* Brahman.
> *This will give you salvation.*[12]

In the above passage and elsewhere too Bhīmā Bhoi talks of something akin to the *aparokṣānubhūti* of Śaṅkara. He also uses

---

[10] *Stuti-Cintāmaṇi*, 88th *bolī*.

[11] *Bhajanamālā*, II.201.

[12] Ibid., I.38.

another term frequently, *santic,* i.e. *a-sādhanā-mārga, ana-sādhanā mārga.* According to the literature of Odisha *a-sādhanā* means the highest yogic stage when the truth is realized transcending all physical and mental states. It is beyond knowledge. Bhīmā Bhoi also uses the word *a-mana,* i.e. transcending the mental propensities. When a *bhakta* truly realizes his own self he attains the *jñāna* through direct experience. Thus he writes:

> *When I talked of* śūnya *everybody fled in fear,*
> *For they could not see anything.*
> *He* (Śūnya-Brahman) *resides in the temple that mind one cannot*
> *reach* (a-mana mandira)
> *He can only be realized by direct experience.*[13]

Jñāna flows spontaneously out of the realization of identity between *ātman* and *paramātman.* There seems to be no dividing line between the terms *jñāna* and *bhakti* as *bhakti* does not have usual connotation associated with the term. If on the one hand it is closely connected with *jñāna,* then it is also equally connected with sense of surrendering the ego that necessitates moral perfection.

So in Mahimā conception of *bhakti* there is no place for elaborate rituals or offering prayers to an idol. It very broadly means fervently yearning for self-realization through the grace of the Almighty. It requires total surrender to the Lord Supreme. Once one attains the truth that there is no distinction between *jīvātman* and *paramātman,* on the one hand, and no discrimination between *Brahman* and the universe on the other, a man realizes the greatness of this power and totally surrenders his empirical ego to it. This is called *bhakti.* Thus by surrendering the egotism, one becomes a true devotee. God becomes not only the object of every action but he is also to be taken as the real agent of all actions. Such actions have no trace of ego. Thus all actions become the veritable offering at the altar of the *alekha mahimā.* Bhīmā Bhoi has again and again emphasized on dedicating life, soul, actions (both good and bad), love of the near and dear ones, at the feet of the Almighty. But in Mahimā Dharma

---

13 *Brahma-Nirūpaṇa Gītā,* III.

bhakti does not just mean self-surrender but much more. This is obvious from the atypical term Bhīmā Bhoi uses in his works, viz. *niṣkāma-bhakti*. In this case *bhakti* is a much more inclusive concept that not only includes spirituality, but also morality and human action in the social context. So to understand the true depth of the Mahimā theory of *bhakti,* we need to discuss briefly the concept of *niṣkāma-bhakti*.

Interestingly, in Mahimā Dharma the development of moral value is taken within the ambience of *bhakti*. For Mahimā Dharma *bhakti* and *jñāna*, though complementary, are futile without *sadguṇa* (perfect qualities). The inculcation of humane qualities like truth, peace, self-control, mercy and non-violence is the first step towards self-realization. One has to be a perfect human being before one becomes fit for indulging in *bhakti*.

The Concept of Niṣkāma-Bhakti: The Progress from Morality to Spirituality

One of the greatest contributions of the Mahimā-panthīs, especially Bhīmā Bhoi, is the concept of *niṣkāma-bhakti*. Very broadly speaking, *bhakti* can be categorized as *sakāma-bhakti* and *niṣkāma-bhakti*. *Sakāma-bhakti* is motivated by desire for something, material or spiritual. But in the case of *niṣkāma-bhakti* it is not treated as a means of attaining something; it is even free of desire for *mukti*. There are many religious treatises that eulogize such an idea of self-realization. For example, *Bhāgavata Purāṇa* talks of such a *bhakti* as *projjita kitaba* (free from all sorts of desire, including that of *mukti*).[14] But Mahimā Dharma offers a unique interpretation of *niṣkāma-bhakti* that only signifies desireless self-surrender to the Highest Principle but also moral perfection. We rarely come across a conceptual analysis of *bhakti* in terms of moral perfection. In fact, according to Mahimā Dharma, moral perfection and *bhakti* have the same connotation. Bhīmā Bhoi dedicates one section of his famous metaphysical work *Brahma-Nirūpaṇa Gītā* in explaining elaborately what *Brahman-bhakti*,

---

[14] However, *Bhāgavata* dismisses the idea of *nirguṇa-bhakti* as well as the idea of the identity between *jīva* and *Parama-Īśvara*.

i.e. *niṣkāma-bhakti* means. I am offering a summary of his explication of the true significance of the term.

> The nature of *Brahman-bhakti* is really unique. Let your heart be full of peace, gentleness, compassion and forgiveness. Let not anger in any form seize your mind, for anger demolishes all *jñāna*. Let you be like mother earth, ever tolerant. As rainwater falls on everything that comes in its way without making discrimination whether it is pleasant or unpleasant; as sunlight brightens everything whether it smells good or bad; as wind blows through every possible space; you also become all-encompassing without making any discrimination between the high-born and low-born, between rich and poor. Any form of discrimination between man and man on the basis of caste and creed leads to *adharma*.[15]
>
> When the mind is free from all such moral imperfections then only can you envision the Supreme Reality.[16]

Mahimā Dharma is otherwise known as Satya Mahimā Dharma. Truthfulness is regarded as the benchmark of true *bhakti*. So Bhīmā Bhoi emphatically states:

> *Bathe in truth,*
> *May you feed yourself on truth.*
> *Your actions,*
> *If pure and true,*
> *Will please the Lord.*
>
> *Whatever you do*
> *Sleep, sit or indulge in your profession,*
> *Be truthful.*
> *This will make the followers of Mahimā great.*
>
> *In speech, in action,*
> *In all your activities*
> *Be truthful.*[17]

---

15 *Brahma-Nirūpaṇa Gītā*, XIV.

16 *niṣkāma hoile mana dr̥śya hebe bhagavāna* – *Bhajanamālā*, II.73.

17 *Stuti-Cintāmaṇi*, 82.

Thus *bhakti* is *niṣkāma* when a *bhakta* is morally well-equipped. This alone makes one spiritually ready for encompassing the society and the universe within one's field of activity. *Bhakti* is not person-centric. One must realize that a human being is but non-different from the universe. Unlike the common norms of practice in which it is thought that true realization comes when one escapes from the din and bustle of the world, Mahimā Dharma insists that the world itself is the seat of self-realization. One must see the whole universe within him. *Niṣkāma-bhakti* does not make one a recluse but a complete social being who identifies himself with the society. According to Bhīmā Bhoi this is the essential character of a *bhakta*. So he says:

> *The identifying mark of a* bhakta *is that he is not limited by any* guṇa (nirguṇa)
> *He considers the mankind as his own brethren and a part of his soul.*[18]

In this context I feel it necessary to clear one misconception that is likely to present a very wrong assessment of the very lofty theory of *ātma-bhakti* or *brahma-jñāna*. Eschmann, following Western norms, calls it "occult doctrine".[19] The entire conception may appear quite queer to a Western mind; and thus they may fail to grasp the true essence of *ātma-jñāna* and *Brahman-bhakti*. But there is nothing secretive or mystical about the concept. We must remember that *ātma-jñāna* as a concept is not only the part and parcel of the Upaniṣadic doctrine, but also many systems of accredited philosophy, including many forms of santic philosophy. In fact, *ātmānam viddhi*, i.e. know thyself, is one of the basic mottos of Upaniṣads. True, these concepts do not come within the scope of a logic or dialectic but that does not make them occult. This is an ideal

---

18 *Stuti-Cintāmaṇi*, 41.

19 A. Eschmann, 1978, "Mahimā Dharma: An Autochthonous Hindu Reform Movement", in H. Kulke and G.C. Tripathi (eds.), *The Cult of Jagannath and the Regional Tradition of Orissa*, New Delhi: Manohar, p. 390.

that ultimately aims at seeing universe within oneself; and oneself in the universe. This is *ātma-jñāna.* In fact, Bhīmā Bhoi is quite clear and open about what is expected in the case of *bhakti* as a form of *ātma-jñāna*. It is in no way secretive and nor is his theory meant for a select few as is the charateristic mark of occult doctrines. He has highlighted again and again on an inclusive view of the humanity as the mark of *bhakti* and also *jñāna.* Similarly, the use of the word esoterism does not apply to all passages and verses of Bhīmā Bhoi. Only in certain chapters of *Nirveda Sādhanā* and *Brahma-Nirūpaṇa Gītā* he talks tantric and yogic practices of different plexus in the body and the way to activate them. But in general he is quite straightforward about the basic philosophical concepts he expounds. Thus we would be doing injustice to the lofty ideals of Mahimā Dharma if we perceive it as "occultism" or "esoterism".

Niṣkāma-Bhakti and Human Action

Before I conclude this chapter I must make it clear that though Mahimā Dharma highlights on *jñāna-bhakti,* yet it does not discard the role of *karma* (action) as an important preliminary for the *bhakti*. According to Bhīmā Bhoi a man cannot exist without doing anything. So he does not preach passivism. He does not ask people to give up the activities of life for the sake of the path of self-realization (*mukti*). Rather he insists on leading a life based on appropriate action:

> *Those who shun actions think that they have achieved peace*
> *But are they going to spend their whole life thus?*
> *Such people are ignorant and unwise*
> *And are under the spell of* māyā.[20]

In this case too Bhīmā Bhoi uses the concept of *niṣkāma* to show that all actions do not lead to bondage. By surrendering the sense of doership one can exercise complete non-attachment. Almost in the spirit of *Bhagavad-Gītā* he advises that while engaged in the activities of life one must surrender the agentship to the Reality Supreme. But again the nature of this highest principle itself is *niṣkāma*. No

---

20 *Stuti-Cintāmaṇi*, 55.

activity done in the name of God can be *sakāma*. So the way to attain it is *niṣkāma*. This does not necessarily mean renouncing the normal activities of life including the actions associated with one's profession. It is the activities of life that bind the society and life together. So, he very justifiably argues:

> If everybody would think of leaving their own profession who else would do his job? If you are devoted to the Lord, in whatever profession you be, *Brahman* would definitely save you.[21]

Elaborating this further he writes:

> *Let the king remain in his seat of power*
> *And carry out administration*
> *May he worship* alekha *in the heart*
> *And dispense justice.*[22]

Here we come across a theory of *sva-dharma* in a different form. He considers the society to be a functional organization and all functions that are essential for its development should be regarded as equal. No action is higher or more valuable than others. This is why he says:

> *Let the cobbler cut and polish the leather*
> *May he take refuge in the name of the Lord.*
> *How can he leave his profession?*
> *Let him earn his daily bread.*[23]

Karma performed in consonance with *dharma* leads one to the highest goal. In other words as long as one performs action with the sense of agenthood, one is bound by the fetters of *saṁsāra*. The suspension of egohood leads to *niṣkāma-karma* as it is but a corollary to *niṣkāma-bhakti*.

Thus we find that according to Mahimā Dharma the concept *niṣkāma* is the prerequisite for all types of *sādhanā*, i.e. the path to spiritual goal. So Bhīmā Bhoi prescribes *niṣkāma-karma*, *niṣkāma-*

---

[21] *Stuti-Cintāmaṇi*, 91.

[22] Ibid., 90.

[23] Ibid.

jñāna and *niṣkāma-bhakti* as the ideals of life, for, when the element of desire (*kāma*) guides the human, life all talks of *dharma, karma* and *mukti* are of no avail.

In the philosophy of Mahimā Dharma one discovers a unique synthesis of *jñāna, karma* and *bhakti* that is held together by the concept of *niṣkāma*. The traditional dichotomy between *jñāna* and *karma*, on the one hand, and *jñāna* and *bhakti*, on the other, does not hold here. These are not exclusive paths leading to *mukti* but all paths are complementary to each other. This is evident from the following *bhajana* of Bhīmā Bhoi:

> *If you make your mind free of desires* (niṣkāma),
> *You can reach that goal.*
> *If you turn yourself to be the servant of servant*
> *Then only can you realize the true essence of* jñāna.[24]

Thus we note a unique amalgamation of individual and social perfection through the path of *bhakti*. This is evident from Bhīmā Bhoi's line "turn yourself to be the servant of servant". In this sense the Mahimā conceptions of *bhakti* and *mukti* are unique and unparalleled.

The Concept of Guru

A look at Bhīmā Bhoi's compositions reveals that very often he advises total surrender, total devotion to *guru*. Sometimes he complains about his sufferings, agonies and frustrations to *guru*. Again sometimes he pleads for his mercy as the saviour and protector. Surprisingly, in certain verses he uses *guru* as well as *Anādi Puruṣa/alekha mahimā* almost interchangeably. This might create a confusion in the mind of the readers regarding the true object of devotion, i.e. whether he accepts his Guru Mahimā Svāmī to be the Ultimate Reality or he refers to some other Reality Supreme? In Indian tradition, right from the Upaniṣadic age, *guru* has been offered a special status as the spiritual guide. Sometimes, it appears that Bhīmā Bhoi uses the term *guru* to refer to Mahimā Svāmī as

---

[24] *Bhajanamālā*, I.78.

the anthropomorphic form of *alekha mahimā Para-Brahman*. But in metaphysical works like *Brahma-Nirūpaṇa Gītā*, *Śrutiniṣedha Gītā* he does not. This fact adds more strength to the confusion. According to S.C. Panigrahi, Bhīmā Bhoi does not always mean by *guru* an embodied person.

> For him, the ultimate reality or *mahimā* is both the knowledge per se and the ultimate knower or the *guru*. For him the spiritual guide is no longer a human being.[25]

He is formless (*anākāra*), formless bliss (*arūpānanda*), *alekha* and *śūnya*; the *guru* is stated to reside in the ultimate *śūnya* having no specific description whatsoever. So his frequent reference to *guru* does not stand for an anthropomorphic form. The clarification with regard to this confusion is perhaps most lucidly offered by Karunakara Sahu, an ardent follower and erudite scholar of Mahimā Dharma, in his editorial Introdution to the collected works of Bhīmā Bhoi.[26] According to him *guru* is offered a status of reverence in Indian tradition. But in Satya Mahimā Dharma the concept of *guru* is posited at a higher level. This *dharma* does not take the word in a narrow sense to mean an embodied person. According to this religion *Prabhu Para-Brahman* is the only *guru* and the primal *guru*. The chief objective of this *dharma* is to bring about a union between the individual self and the Supreme Self. In this sense *Para-Brahman* is also called *Guru-Brahman*. Thus we notice that Bhīmā Bhoi with an unprecedented ease addresses Gurudeva Svāmī, as *nirguṇa-puruṣa*, *niṣkāma-puruṣa*, *arūpānanda* and also as *śūnya-dehī* (*śūnya*-bodied) who resides in the temple of *śūnya*. Such an explanation can be corroborated by the fact that Mahimā-panthīs neither worship any image or symbol of the *guru* as it happens in case of innumerable *guru*-centric cults in India. During their morning prayer known as *śaraṇa darśana* the Mahimā-panthīs only chant *mahimā alekha Para-Brahman* and nothing else.

---

25 S.C. Panigrahi, 1998, *Bhīmā Bhoi and Mahimā Darśana*, Bhubaneswar: D.S.A. in Philosophy, Utkal University, p. 52.

26 K.K. Sahu, 2000, *Bhaktakabi Bhīmā Bhoi Granthāvali*, Cuttack: Dharma Grantha Store.

7

The Dissident Stream of Spirituality

IN my introductory chapter I made it clear that the post-Classical philosophy (that is often branded as Bhakti movement) is non-conformist in attitude. It defied some of the basic presumptions of the so-called orthodox tradition. Yet this group of thinkers cannot be labelled as "outsiders". They were the dissidents who wanted to chart out a new path discarding all that rotted the society in general. Mahimā Dharma is virtually one of the latest symbols of this trend. Though often wrongly allied to Buddhism or Christianity, it was very much a part of the tradition. In the words of A. Eschmann, a renowned scholar on Mahimā Dharma, "this movement derives its criticism of the Hindu tradition directly from the tradition itself, thus standing in an almost paradoxical twofold relation to the tradition which it accepts on the one hand, and rejects on the other".[1] Thus Mahimā Dharma could be labelled as a philosophy of dissent. Before we go into the details of its attitude to the orthodox tradition let us briefly scan the nature of the dissident stream of spirituality. I feel it necessary to dwell on the issue as it might be helpful in providing some insight into Mahimā Dharma and its place in the history of ideas.

The dissident stream of spirituality is not exactly something strange as far as the history of Indian cultural and spiritual tradition is concerned. Indian cultural heritage represents a wonderful potential to accommodate the voice of dissent. In fact, the so-called orthodox and the anti-orthodox trends seem to move in a parallel

---

[1] A. Eschmann, 1978, "Mahimā Dharma: An Autochthonous Hindu Reform Movement", in H. Kulke and G.C. Tripathi (eds.) *The Cult of Jagannath and Regional Traditions of Orissa*, Delhi: Manohar, p. 375.

line throughout the development of the Indian philosophical, religious and cultural tradition. If the Vedic tradition was respected and held to be dominant then those who voiced scepticism about its authenticity were never discouraged. So occasionally we come across the names of Lokāyatas, Ājīvakas, Sañjaya, the sceptic and Anuvādins. However, our dominant Brāhmanical tradition as well as the later academicians have all along been eloquent in their silence about such non-Vedic trends. As Amartya Sen very rightly points out:

> Recognizing the history of heterodoxy in India is critically important for coming to grips with the cross-current of ideas, including intellectual processes and scrutinized convictions, that have survived through the turbulence and turmoil of Indian history. Underestimation of heterodoxy which, alas, is far too common can prevent an adequate understanding of Indian tradition.[2]

Unfortunately the cultural predominance of the so-called Vedic tradition (or is it Brāhmanism?) continues to be the driving force of our modern scholasticism. So, virtually very little information is passed on to the posterity about dissident streams of thought.

> That selective inattention has, in fact, produced a substantial bias in the interpretation of Indian thought, and through that in the understanding of the intellectual heritage of contemporary India.[3]

The "selective inattention" of the scholars not only applies to the voice of dissidence from outside the Vedic tradition but also the voice from within the tradition.

The Dissident Stream of Spirituality

If we look at whatever scanty material is available on the non-Vedic tradition, especially the Śramaṇic tradition, then we note that there is a common tendency of dismissing the two pillars of the Vedic

---

[2] Amartya Sen, 2005, *The Argumentative Indian: Writing on Indian Culture, History and Identity*, London: Penguin Books, 2005, p. 21.

[3] Ibid., p. 25.

tradition, viz. the predominance of the rituals, including animal and human sacrifice; and the division of the society along the caste lines, famously known as *varṇa-dharma*. Mahimā Dharma is one of the latest movements in the Indian history of ideas to challenge these two pillars of Hindu orthodoxy. The Lokāyatas, believed to be one of the oldest dissident streams of thought, was quite vociferous about these two elements of the Vedic and post-Vedic traditions. Even within the texts of Veda we find reference to Bṛhaspati, the pioneer of this school. The Buddhists, Jainas and Ājīvakas, though they did not share materialistic philosophy of the Lokāyatas, were equally explicit in their denial of the Vedic authority and the pattern of life suggested by the orthodox (Vedic) tradition. Buddhism very openly challenged the orthodoxy and orthopraxis of this period. But we must remember that our dominant orthodox tradition has from the very beginning excluded such dissident voice from its own purview by tagging them as the *nāstika*s (generally translated as non-orthodox or non-Vedic). But as I have already stated, around thirteenth century CE (even earlier) there was a renewed attempt to defy the hegemony of the orthodoxy, that later on came to be known as the Bhakti movement. It had its genesis in the south and turned into a pan-Indian movement during thirteenth to nineteenth centuries. Here, however, I do not intend to provide a sketch of the history of the dissident stream of spirituality in Indian philosophical tradition. I would rather concentrate on some of the issues that have acted as catalysts for such forms of dissent.

Anybody dealing with the development of the religio-philosophical history of India would note that the so-called Vedic or orthodox tradition has always supported an elitist domination of the society. One can easily find that a deep gulf was all along maintained between the privileged and the underprivileged, between the so-called polluted people and the pure.

Dharma and the Children of Lesser God

Social stratification on the basis of birth largely shaped and till date continues to determine what has been accepted as sacrosanct by the average followers of Hinduism. Despite intermittent challenges the orthopraxis of the Vedic tradition (or whatever is passed in the name of Vedic tradition) continues unabated. The dominance of the Dharmaśāstras, that was believed to be the only available guide for a life of *dharma*, gradually led to the class-based hierarchical division of the society along with the uncontested supremacy of the brāhmaṇas as a class. What was just hinted at in the Puruṣa-Sūkta of *R̥gveda* about the origin of different classes of people from different limbs of *Puruṣa* became an inviolable theory of social hierarchy famously known as *varṇa-dharma*. Ironically, generations of Indians have no idea of what is contained in Vedas but they are strict adherents of caste distinction that divides the society into four classes – brāhmaṇa, kṣatriya, vaiśya and śūdra – with śūdra being placed in the lowest rung of the social hierarchy. To this was later on added another class who were taken as untouchables. Purāṇas that were composed in later phases very faithfully followed the tenets of Dharma-Śāstras. I shall take some sample *Kārikās* from *Manu Saṁhitā* to illustrate to what extent the atrocious discrimination between the higher caste and lower caste became the part of the *dharma*. According to Manu, brāhmaṇas (highest class in the social ladder) should be treated as next to God. He ordains:

> Since brāhmaṇa sprang from the most excellent part, since he has the priority arising from the primogeniture and since he possesses Veda, he is by right the lord (*Prabhu*) of this whole creation.
>
> – I.93

> A brāhmaṇa, whether learned or unlearned, is a mighty divinity (*daivatam mahat*), just as fire is a mighty divinity, whether consecrated or unconsecrated. – X.317

But when it comes to the lowest rung of the society, viz. śūdra, Manu makes it clear:

> Only one work did the lord ordain for the śūdras is to ungrudgingly serve the three higher castes. – I.11

Thus in every respect members of the śūdra class were regarded as the children of a lesser God with very few social and cultural rights.

According to Manu, śūdras are *ekajanma* (once-born) in contrast to the other three castes, viz. brāhmaṇa, kṣatriya, vaiśya, who are *dvija* (twice-born) (X.4). The three higher classes, brāhmaṇas, kṣatriyas and vaiśyas are twice-born (*dvija*), because first time they are biologically born and the second time they are culturally born. The second birth is metaphorical and it may be called initiation in the process of culturalization that is done during their studentship under the *guru* (teacher). The śūdra, on the other hand, is not allowed to undergo such ceremonies, and therefore, he is born only once (*ekajanma*). Let us look at the implications of such a distinction.

> Since such ceremonies of culturalization were held in schools under the guru's direction, by implication the śūdra and other so-called lower castes were not allowed to be admitted in any school, i.e. they were not allowed to be formally educated.[4]

This explains why a śūdra or a member of the untouchable class is not allowed to read Vedas. Since he is not educated where is the question of his having the knowledge of Vedas or the finer aspects of life? The subsequent sacred texts like *Bhāgavata Purāṇa* ordains that śūdras should be treated as the lowliest in the social ladder as they by very nature are impure (*apabitra*).[5] There are many scholars who still defend that *varṇa-vyavasthā* is not caste distinction and most often fail to show what should be the basis of discrimination between man and man. Is it human nature (*svabhāvaja*)? Certainly not. So we are grateful to S. Radhakrishnan who frankly admits:

> Since in each individual case we cannot determine what the aptitudes of the individual are, heredity and training are used to fix the calling.[6]

I shall not go into the details of this shameful tradition that is

---

[4] Rajendra Prasad, 1999, *Varṇadharma, Niṣkāma Karma and Practical Morality*, Bhubaneswar: Department of Special Assistance in Philosophy, p. 8.

[5] *Bhāgavata Purāṇa*, Skanda XI, chap. 17.

[6] S. Radhakrishnan, 1976, *The Hindu View of Life*, Bombay: Allen & Unwin, p. 79.

perpetuated till date, though we have forgotten what Manu or even *Bhāgavata Purāṇa* actually means by *dharma*.

The second trend that had its origin in the Smṛtis like the Dharmaśāstras gave emphasis on rituals. In fact, *Manu Saṁhitā* that is most often accepted as the authentic scripture for the Hindu way of life deals primarily with *saṁskāra*s or rituals from the very stage of conception to death. All such rituals are entirely brāhmaṇa-centric, as such rituals could only be performed by none other than the brāhmaṇas. This gave rise to the dependence of the society on the brahmaṇas for the performance of the prescribed rituals associated with different phases of life. This feature of our *dharma* has taken such a deep root in our psyche that we cannot do without this. When we come to the realities of twenty-first century we notice that even if our lifestyle has changed, even if we have adopted more or less the Western modes of life, the elements of brāhmaṇa-centrism enunciated by Smṛtis and Purāṇas continue to be the most dominating force in our society. It goes on unabated. No religious ceremony seems to be complete without being presided over by a brāhmaṇa, even if he pronounces *mantra*s wrongly; even if he does not understand a word of what he mutters. How many of our enlightened ilk can perform a funeral rite or any other rite associated with the life of a Hindu without soliciting the services of a priest? The very act of dissent is regarded as *adharma*. After the practice of idol worship became a part of our orthodox tradition, our conception of *dharma* gradually was enmeshed in the elaborate growth of institutionalism, organized priesthood, rigid codification and sectarianism. People started believing that visit to temples, performance of rites, offering fee for the worship to the priests, pilgrimage and other religious duties would earn for them spiritual dividend. In most of such activities the brāhmaṇa class played an important role, and in the process usurped the right of other castes to be closer to God. This privileged class is still in no mood to share their God with the underprivileged. There are many temples in India that do not allow the śūdras to enter the precincts of the temple.

Bhakti as a Form of Non-Conformism

The dissident movement that is most often labelled as the Bhakti movements is definitely a landmark in the intellectual and cultural tradition of India. Though accepting the common tenets of the orthodox world-view like the faith in *karma, ātman*, rebirth and the reality of God Supreme, this new movement challenged all that had so far passed in the name of *dharma*, like rituals, caste discrimination and supremacy of the elite class. The champions of this movement almost changed the vocabulary of the concept of *dharma* as well as *bhakti*. For them *bhakti* stood for a form of the experience of the Supreme Being rather than following the path prescribed by the sacred texts. In this case the love of God became the supreme concern, not merits (*puṇya*) or demerits (*pāpa*). For them the rituals, priesthood, the way of life sanctioned by the Smr̥ti texts held no significance. They brought down spirituality from the upper echelons to the heat and dust of common life. Elements like caste and creed, polluted and pure, rites and the so-called religious duties, forms and icons, Vedas and Śāstras did not have any significance for them. The word *bhakti* became their main conceptual tool for challenging orthodox social mores. *Bhakti* is now presented as a state of heart and soul that transcends the barrier of caste, rituals and other frills associated with religion. *Bhakti* as signifying pure and unalloyed love turned into an apparatus encompassing the whole humanity within its fold. Here God is seen as the all-pervading principle that permeates everything and being. He is no longer confined to the idols and modes of worship associated with the propitiation of God. No doubt, *Bhāgavata Purāṇa*, that is often thought to be the source of what we now call Hinduism, has highlighted the element of love as a means of *bhakti*. There are, no doubt, scattered lines that talk of the equality of man in the eyes of God. But in the final analysis it could not come out of the safe confines of the caste-based social system that was taken as most sacrosanct by our orthodox tradition.

The idea of *bhakti* as love that includes within its scope the ideal of human equality could be noted for the first time in sixth-seventh century CE in the works and practice of the Vaiṣṇava Āḷvārs and the Śaiva Nāyanmārs of the south India. In every sense this can be said to be the beginning of a parallel form of spiritualism that tried to raise its voice, though not explicitly, but in subtler way to change the way of looking at God as well as the humanity. The most important shift they initiated was to remove the barrier that separated God from the common people. The Āḷvārs wrote in a language that was a mixture of Tamil and Sanskrit. Thus spirituality could come down to the commonest of the common. The second important phenomenon that makes this movement a path-breaker in the Indian religio-spiritual tradition was the transfer of gravitation from the Brāhmanical supremacy to the universality of human brotherhood. What is most noteworthy is that the Āḷvārs were not necessarily drawn from the upper caste. They hailed from the different sections of the community stretching from brāhmaṇas to *harijans*. Tiruppan, one of the famous Āḷvārs, was a *harijan*. Besides the mode of their expression was through the lilting lyrics composed in vernacular language that could make it more appealing to the common folks. These features became the hallmark of the Bhakti movement that resurfaced thirteenth century onwards. Their form of spirituality was not bound by the rules of Śāstras. One may not find a strict and systematic exposition or metaphysics in their writings. But their poetic expressions had enough materials to drive directly into the heart of people the real meaning of God realization, for, their tool was experience, not speculation. Their aim was to free the spiritual and religious experience from the bonds of Purāṇic ideologies and supposedly inviolable social structures. A closer look shows that their writings underpinned a well-delineated system of thought in which God is conceived both as ineffable yet an immanent reality, I cite here a few lines from Nammāḷvār the famous Āḷvār to highlight their conception of God as well as the relation between God and the universe.

He is everything
He is everyone
He is and is not

In the religions they have
He does not admit of being spoken
By the five senses
He is known by one's consciousness
He takes from there.[7]

These lines speak of the ineffability and all-pervasiveness of God who need not be propitiated through *mantra*s and rituals but has to be experienced in the innermost consciousness. We notice a similar attitude to God, man and the society in the works the Śaiva *siddha*s of Tamil Nadu. These spiritual leaders predominated the religio-sociological scene sometime between third to fifth century CE. Very much like the Āḷvārs they tried to bring the common people within the fold of enlightenment with the theory of *bhakti*. Thirumular, one of the pioneers of this school of thought, puts forward in simple language the central message of *dharma*, viz. "Love is God". So he says:

Senseless are those who say
Love and Śiva are two
They know not
It is love that becomes Śiva.[8]

The other eminent *siddha*s of this school emphasized with a new vigour that all men are equal. Naturally they denounced the caste system and discouraged idol worship, and also condemned all forms of ritualism. They laid stress on meditation upon the indwelling God as the means of self-realization. Though most of them use the word Śiva to denote God, their religion is universal and undenominational. So they claim:

To the one family doth mankind belong,
And its God
Is one

---

7 Quoted in *Devotional Poets and Mystics*, Delhi: Ministry of Information & Broadcasting, Government of India, 1991, p. 30.

8 Ibid., p. 1.

And one only.[9]

Śivavakkiar, another *siddha* of this order, therefore does not hesitate to condemn idol worship and strongly states:

You plant a stone,
Throw a few flowers over it.
Go round it,
And mutter some mantras,
When Lord is inside you.
Can the planted stones speak?
Can the pot taste the food it has cooked?
Or the laddle.[10]

We notice that despite the dominance of the Purāṇic conception of God the idea of *bhakti* had already become an instrument of egalitarianism as early as fifth-sixth century CE. The innovative idea of *bhakti* had already paved the way for a new approach to God realization that was not bound by the shackles of social hierarchy, rigid rituals and constricted conception of God. During ninth century Kashmir Śaivism not only depicted God as *śūnya* (ineffable one) but it too defied the authority of Vedas and didn't believe in caste system, ceremonial worship and rituals. The same attitude is reflected in the thought and practice of the Vīraśaivas during twelfth century. They outrightly rejected the traditional caste hierarchy and staunchly believed in the equality of men and women. Oppressed and downtrodden people received special attention from them.

In the thirteenth century again the trend was revived and almost swept the Indian spiritual scene. That was the period when Islam gained some ground in India. This perhaps made the traditionalists more insecure about their religious autonomy. Strict orthodoxy and adherence to ritualism, sanctioned by the Dharmaśāstras bounced back in the society. So it was left to the free spirits and the lovers of humanity to create a congenial atmosphere of spirituality. Thus

---

9 Quoted in *Devotional Poets and Mystics*, p. 15.

10 Ibid.

there was a resurgence of Bhakti movement. Our religious world-view got a boost from a series of *sant*s who preached a religion of love and humanism. There was an uninterrupted stream of this dissident form of philosophy till we come to the last part of the nineteenth century. The *bhakti* philosophy that had dominated the south some 600 years back revived with a new vengeance. Thinkers like Kabīr, Ravidāss and Rajjab brought a new wave of hope for the downtrodden and especially the so-called polluted people. All these great *sant*s flourished in the fifteenth century and had a large number of followers. The members of the sects established by them are still very active. But it was Kabīr who was largely responsible for the popularity of the Bhakti movement in the north.

Kabīr, as is well known, was drawn from the backward community of the weavers. He was in fact unlettered yet very few *ācārya*s could equal him in the revolutionary idea that he propagated about the religio-spiritual craving of man. Like the Tamil *bhakta*s he substituted experience for speculation. Very much like the Āḷvārs and Nāyanmārs he spoke of God in the language of love. His God was the God of love and mercy – not the unconditioned God of the Advaita Vedānta – but a Lord of one's heart. So he decried all that had crumpled the traditional view of religion, including idol worship, rituals, blind faith in the scriptures. In fact, he very frankly admitted his disdain for the emissaries of the traditional religion in the following words:

How can there be a meeting of mind between you and me?
For, whatever I say is drawn from my direct experience.
But yours is drawn from the papers (sacred scriptures).[11]

Similarly, Rajjab observed:

> The universe is Veda, the creation is the Koran. The *puṇḍits* and *kāẓīs* are deceived when they think that the whole world is encompassed within the dry books. The heart of the worshipper is the page on which the story of the universal truth is written in

---

[11] *The Bījak of Kabīr*, tr. into English by Linda Hess and Sukhdev Singh, Motilal Banarsidass, repr. edn., 2001, p. 90.

letters of life. . . . Why do you waste your time on dead books?[12]

Kabīr and the thinkers of his time expressed the experienced wisdom about God, the nature of the world and the universal brotherhood through powerful lyrics in the language of the people. Like all other thinkers of this genre they saw the humanity as a large family. For most of such *sant*s God is an inexplicable reality who pervades and permeates the whole universe as butter permeates milk. So God is all-pervasive yet non-personalized. One has to realize him within. But Kabīr's poems were hard-hitting. Let us look at the following lines of Kabīr:

To tonsured monks and dreadlocked rasa
To idol worshippers and idol smashers,
To fasting Jains and feasting Śaivites,
To Vedic puṇḍits *and Faber poets,*

The weaver Kabir sends one message:
The noose of death hangs over all.
Only Rama's name can save you.
Say in NOW.[13]

Again, we mark the same note of revolt against Brāhmanical way of treating a large section of society as "untouchables", in the following poem.

Puṇḍit, *look in your heart of knowledge.*
Tell me where untouchability
Came from since you believe in it.

xx *xx* *xx*

We eat by touching, we wash by touching,
from touch the world was born.
So who is untouched? Asks Kabīr.

---

[12] Quoted in, Ksitimohan Sen, 1983, "Medieval Mystics of North India", in *The Cultural Heritage of India*, Calcutta: Ramkrisha Mission, p. 386.

[13] Mehrotra, A.K. (tr.), 2011, *Songs of Kabir*, New York: NYRB Classics, p. 29.

Who is untouched by māyā.[14]

These lines clearly show Kabīr's mistrust for all that spoil the pure spirituality of that human beings pine to achieve.

The *sant*s of Odisha were no less rebellious as far as idolatry and caste discrimination were concerned. The Pañcasakhā group of *sant*s proudly declared themselves as śūdra, though in fact, most of them belonged to the higher caste. According to them unless one develops the aptitude of śūdra, i.e. serving others without a trace of ego one cannot be a true *bhakta*. This is otherwise known as śūdra-*bhakti*. So they dreamt of a casteless and classless society. I cite here one example. Acyutānanda Dāsa in one of his works makes Kṛṣṇa say:

> Well did you ask, O Arjuna! about the status of a scavenger. I tell you he is not distinct from me.[15]

Thus we notice that the Indian philosophical tradition has always accommodated the spirit of dissidence, otherwise the *sant*s like Kabīr, Rajjab and Ravidāss, Thirumular or the Pañcasakhā of Odisha could not have come out so forcefully against the social discrimination and religious pomposities. This is rather unfortunate that the academic scholars usually take resort to what I stated as "selective amnesia". This becomes clear from the fact that despite voluminous works written on Hinduism during the last fifty years, including the very famous ones, there is a total blank about the contributions made by these dissenters of the orthodoxy.

Mahimā Dharma and the Voice of Dissent

The Mahimā Dharma that came to the fore in the last part of the nineteenth century CE was the continuation of this revolutionary spiritual journey. Of course, the *sant*s of Odisha, especially, Pañcasakhā and their followers, had been quite vociferous in decrying the ritualistic interpretation of *dharma* and idol worship,

---

[14] Quoted from the English translation of poems of Kabīr, in Linda Hess and Sukhdev Singh, 2001, *The Bījak of Kabīr*, Delhi: Motilal Banarsidass, p. 55.

[15] Acyutānanda Dāsa, *Kaivarta Gītā*.

but Mahimā Dharma was much more rebellious in its attitude. Its voice of dissent came from within the heart as the society during that period had witnessed the worst forms of atrocities and ignominy meted out to the marginalized section of the society in the name of Sanātana Dharma. So when Mahimā Svāmī, the founder of the *dharma* came out with the revolutionary idea of no idol, no caste distinction, no religious pomposities, but a simple life of surrendering to the One and ineffable *Alekha Mahimā* it ignited a new hope in the heart of the people who have been treated as pariahs. The movement perhaps took the shortest time to spread across different parts of Odisha. It was a *dharma* of the outcastes; of the people who had quite for some time suffered the humiliation perpetuated by the nexus of the royalty and elite class. Bhīmā Bhoi was the child of his times who had suffered the pangs of disgrace. Often he has been derided as a "Kandha", the tribal. The agony of being treated as lowly therefore finds expression while presenting the rebellious spirit of Mahimā Dharma. In his compositions there is no trace of compromise. Rather it is ruthless in its assault against the orthodox view of *dharma*, against the dominance of the higher castes who claimed the exclusive right to spirituality; against the idol worship and the institutionalized forms of religious practices. He had the courage of conviction even to disown the supremacy of Lord Jagannātha who was regarded as the *rāṣṭra-devatā*, the God of the nation; and was the symbol of Odia identity. Bhīmā Bhoi even portrayed Jagannātha as the disciple of the *Alekha Mahimā*. His logic for such a sweeping view was straightforward.

The *sādhu*s and *sant*s say that Lord Jagannātha resides in the grand temple. But had he been the real master of the universe (the etymological meaning of Jagannātha) why should he have confined himself within the precincts of the temple? Why should he have created the discrimination between man and man? He is called Jagannātha because in His eyes everybody in the world is equal.[16]

In another verse he clarifies:

---

[16] *Śrutiniseḍha Gītā*, II.

Jagannātha is within your heart
You unnecessarily worship his idol.
His idol is made after all, with dry wood
Can the worship of such an idol take you to Vaikuṇṭha?[17]

Idols are just made up of five gross elements. Therefore thinking that such idols would be the source of divinity is nothing but ignorance:

Look how ignorant the people are?
They fall at the feet of idols and promise to offer all delicacies
For the fulfilment of their prayer.
They are but statues without consciousness or soul.
How can such a God grant you boons?[18]

Not only did he defy the idolatry, he also strongly believed that the innumerable gods and goddesses worshipped in the temple are no more sacred. The divinity has vanished[19] from all those so-called sacred places as temples had turned into the centre of institutionalized oppression of the poor and the deprived. It must be noted here that Bhīmā Bhoi was not exactly against the Hindu gods and goddesses. In his works we come across many accounts found in Hindu mythology. He even composed a whole series of verse on Jagannātha.[20] His only grudge was against the injustice that was encouraged by the so-called houses of God. So he discarded all that was taken to be source of religious oppression and ritualistic worship, including Vedas and Śāstras. Vedas and Śāstras for him

---

17 *Śrutiniseḍha Gītā*, p. 10.

18 One may note the same tone and tenor in the work of Dvārakā Dāsa, the eighteenth-century Odia *sant*:
They worship others neglecting me
And know not I am the ātman
Making idols of wood, stone and metal
Happy in their ignorance.
– Dvārakā Dāsa, *Parace Gītā*, X

19 *Stuti-Cintāmaṇi*, 95th *bolī*.

20 Ibid., 8th *bolī*.

are "moth-eaten dry leaves".[21]

Bhīmā Bhoi's disdain for Vedas and Śāstras and all social oppression carried out in the name of such texts comes out clearly in the following lines:

> *Many may talk of the reality and show the path narrated by* Śāstras,
> *Without ever knowing what the* Brahman *is.*
> *That is why the experts in Veda are called "drunkard"*
> *The knowledge of* Śāstras *make them more confused.*
> *As a drunkard under the spell of liquor talks without sense,*
> *Similar is the attitude of the people adept in* Śāstras
> *How can they explain the nature of* Brahman?
> *They can go as far as Veda can dictate them not more.*[22]

So in Bhīmā Bhoi's works we very frequently come across the word *nirveda*. In fact, one of his famous treatises is entitled *Nirveda Sādhanā*. In this case *nirveda* means any path of self-realization that transcends Veda:

> *Nirveda* is above the words (text), *nirveda* is above Veda, the formless is above the *nirveda*.[23]

We have discussed earlier how Mahimā Dharma insists on the direct realization of the highest truth. So the texts and scriptures have no role to play for a true seeker. Thus he says:

> Mantra, yantra, tantra *and* sūtra,
> *And Vedic sacrifices, along with Vedānta,*
> *And the sayings of* siddhas, *all were demolished*
> *With the rise of this Dharma.*[24]

---

[21] *cāri veda cāri granthe kita pataṅga je yukta* ।
– *Bhajanamālā*, I.29

[22] *Brahma-Nirūpaṇa Gītā*, 14.127-30.

[23] *śabda upare rahiachi nirveda, veda upare rahiacchi nirveda, nirveda upare achhi aṇākāra* । – *Bhajanamālā*, I.32

[24] *Stuti-Cintāmaṇi*, 55.6.

I entirely agree with Bettina Bäumer when she remarks:

> It is thus more surprising that the Dharma has been completely Vedānticized by Biśvanātha Bābā, which not only goes against Bhīmā Bhoi's thought, but against the whole tenet of Mahimā Dharma.[25]

Again, Bhīmā Bhoi does not find any rationale behind the practice of going pilgrimage. He staunchly believed that God does not exist in any particular place. So every place is a holy place. Bhīmā Bhoi believes that since the human body itself is the seat of God one need not go on long pilgrimages. One need not go to temples to find him. One has to just turn within. God can be served not by sacramental offerings, by rites and rituals in the temples but by serving God's creation, for, God is manifested in every thing and being. A true *dharma* should help people to expand their vision wherein they realize God in His essential nature. So he says:

> *Without knowing the essence of God*
> *You roam all around*
> *For the sake of* tīrtha *and* vrata.
> *If you think deeply,*
> *Then you can see* Brahman,
> *Wherever you want Him.*[26]

He was painfully aware and vehemently critical of the path of ostentation encouraged by the so-called Sanātana Dharma. In later Hinduism elaborate rituals were prescribed for propitiating each and every deity. This appeared funny to Bhīmā Bhoi. He felt that people wasted their precious life in mechanical rites and rituals forgetting that it is only through the realization of the God's presence in the *ātman* that one can achieve *mukti*. In the realization that there is no distinction between God and his manifestation, one can achieve the true realization. Ritualism gives rise to fundamentalism. People mistake the superficiality of religious observances as the essence

---

[25] Bettina Bäumer and Johannes Beltz (eds.), *Bhīmā Bhoi: Verses from the Void*, p. 51.

[26] *Stuti-Cintāmaṇi*, 92th *bolī*.

of religion. According to Bhīmā Bhoi a true religion always aims at empathizing and sympathizing with one's fellowmen. *Stuti-Cintāmaṇi* records how fervently he pleads to the people for the observance of a *dharma* free from rites and rituals, free from religious hypocrisies. But the people of his time were afraid of transgressing the diktat of Śāstras and Purāṇas. So sometimes Bhīmā Bhoi gets so frustrated about the attitude of the people that he gives vent to his anger and impatience in the following words:

The wickedness of the years of Kali
The world grows vicious
Day by day.
For their evil ways and vile traditions
all shall be swept
Away from this world in a flash.[27]

If on the one hand Mahimā Dharma struck at the root of idol worship and meaningless rituals and practices that grew around such faith, on the other, it protested with equal vigour against the system of social hierarchy based on *varṇa-dharma*. The haughtiness of the higher castes had already made the life of major chunk of the society unbearable. So in Bhīmā Bhoi's compositions we come across his angst at the plight of those who belonged to the lowest rung of the society. I have discussed earlier about the historical circumstances in which the people belonging to the lower cadre of the society were treated as less than human beings in Odisha during the nineteenth century CE. Mahimā Svāmī wanted to give these hapless people a place under the sun. His mission was to assure them of their human dignity. This accounted for the mass appeal as well as the popularity of Mahimā Dharma. In the social plane Mahimā Dharma believed in the equality of one and all.

We have noted in the first part of this chapter how the *caturvarṇa* formed the very basis of our socio-cultural tradition. I have also discussed how from time to time the *sant*s have raised their voice against the social order based on *varṇa-dharma*. Odia *sant*s were

---

[27] *Stuti-Cinatāmaṇi*, 26th *bolī*.

no exception to this. In the case of Mahimā Dharma, the defiance becomes more sharp. Mahimā Svāmī and Bhīmā Bhoi were no ordinary social reformers. They were the practical philosophers who intended to offer a metaphysics that a man could live by. So in most cases the protest against social discrimination is strongly backed by metaphysics. If God is One and unique and the world is nothing but the manifestation of the divinity, then everything is divine. Besides, the Mahimā philosophy has whole-heartedly preached the identity between *piṇḍa* and *brahmāṇḍa*. So it logically follows that each individual is potentially divine. So where is the scope for discrimination between man and man? Where is the scope for inequity between the pure and polluted human beings? So they have always believed in the equality of human beings.

Bhīmā Bhoi, following the basic Mahimā tenet, questioned the very conception of such division of human society into *jāti* (caste).

> *"We are of the higher caste"*
> *Thus they vent their shallow arrogance.*
> *All such division of thirty-six classes and fifty-two sub-classes*
> *Are not to be called* jātis.
> *We have created all the divisions*
> *On the basis of who should touch water*
> *From whose house.*
>
> *xx xx xx*
>
> *Do not make any discrimination*
> *Just take refuge in the name of the Lord.*[28]

So he entreats:

> *May you never discriminate between*
> *A* brāhmana *and a* cāṇḍāla
> *May you never bother about* jāti *and* gotra
> *May you never*
> *Conform to the order*

---

[28] *Stuti-Cintāmaṇi*, 70th *bolī*.

Of high and low.[29]

His fervent appeal was based on his conviction that:

You go around the three worlds (brahmāṇḍa)
You will find there is but one humanity and one jāti.
That one humanity created by Him
Is divided into hundred jātis *by the world* (*human beings*).[30]

If at all we have to talk of *jāti* and caste, then there could be only two forms:

God has created only two forms – man and woman.
Apart from these two jātis *O wise man see, there is no third caste.*[31]

What is astounding about Bhīmā Bhoi's conception of equality among human beings is his bold attitude towards women. Right from Dharmaśāstras and Purāṇas to the compositions in vernacular language women are always given a secondary status. But Bhīmā Bhoi sees no real ground for the discrimination between men and women. Giving women an equal status as men is a distinctive phenomenon that is rarely noticed even in the preaching of the *sants*. Some of the most liberal-minded thinkers have not desisted from putting the women at a lower level. In this sense Bhīmā Bhoi is a true rebel who dares to throw away all accepted and deep-rooted social dogmas with a strong logic. He argues:

As the two (men and women)
Emerge from the same power
Both these varṇas *are identical.*
As water and wind do not make any discrimination
In the course of their flow,
The level that a man can go can also be reached by a woman.[32]

xx *xx* *xx*

---

[29] Ibid., 85th *bolī*.

[30] *Stuti-Cintāmaṇi*, 70th *bolī*.

[31] Ibid.

[32] *Brahma-Nirūpaṇa Gītā*, 11.97-98.

When it comes to Brahman-bhakti there is no scope for inequity
Whoever entertains such thought would be in the hell.[33]

Bhīmā Bhoi's conviction about the need for social equality had its roots not only at a conceptual level, it was instigated by the practical experience of his times. He confesses:

Every time
They dare mock me
Bhīmā the lowly Kandha.[34]

Still he proudly referred to himself as Bhīmā – the "Kandha" in many of the colophones of his poems. He still fervently wished to change the attitude of the people towards admitting the caste discrimination.

From door to door I went
And showed them unasked
The path to salvation.
But the dunces said:
Who will accept fare
from all the castes,
And become a Christian?[35]

This is obvious from the lines that at that point of time defying the caste distinction was thought to go against the norms of Hinduism. He sometimes feels so frustrated and agonized by the attitude of the society that he gives vent to his anger.

For me the entire world
With nine continents all,
Is no more than a plate of clay.
To me the whole creation,
With its fifty-six crore living beings,
Looks no better than a piece of straw.
In a single day,

---

33 *Brahma-Nirūpaṇa Gītā*, 103.

34 *Stuti-Cintāmaṇi*, 62th *bolī*.

35 Ibid., quoted from English translation by Siddhartha Satpathy.

I can destroy
The wicked world.
Yet how can I?
I do not have the permission of the revered guru.[36]

And sometimes in desperation he warns like a doomsayer warning of the advent of apocalypse:

Village after village
will fall to ruin.
So will be the fate of rājya *and* deśa.
In the whole hamlet
Only a few will survive
With the name of Mahimā quivering on their lips.

xx xx xx

Let us see at that time,
Which wretched son of a whore
Will cling to his jāti *and* gotra?
Just wait,
We will see how they would observe
The rituals of karma,
And the doctrine of exclusion.[37]

The followers of this *dharma* still offer their prayers to a non-iconic God; and still claim that

> If you search for *mukti* then forget *jāti* (caste), and if you search for *jāti*, then better forget *mukti*.

[36] *Stuti-Cintāmaṇi*, 26th *bolī*.

[37] Ibid., 24th *bolī*.

8

God as Śūnya and Universalism

My main objective of writing this book though primarily is to focus on the novel metaphysical and socio-cultural tenets of Mahimā Dharma, in some sense or other, the very conception of God as *śūnya* forms its axis. All its theories – metaphysical, cosmological, socio-religious – branch off from this point. If God is conceived as *śūnya*, the self-complete principle, then any attempt to describe it disturbs its self-completeness. Hence it is ineffable. Its self-completeness embraces within its fold the whole creation including the man and the varied dimensions of his life. The man under no circumstances can be segregated from the universe, from the society and from the divine. The very Supreme Reality and all that emanate from it are non-different. Naturally, non-difference/equality (*samatā*) is the keyword. So it logically follows that human being self-conscious creatures not only treat every being equally but feels one with every aspect of the creation. This sense of equality leads humans to a sense of compassion for one and all. A true follower of the theory of God as *śūnya* defies the rituals sanctioned by Veda and Śāstras for it leads to discrimination in some form or other between man and God and between man and man. So in most cases, such theories do not highlight the principle of equality. But Mahimā Dharma, being the staunchest adherent of the theory of God as *śūnya,* takes the final logical step by admitting the importance of equality that finally leads to the idea of compassion (*karuṇā*). Universalism is an inherent aspect of Mahimā theory of God as *śūnya*. Mahimā Dharma at no stage asks its followers to distance themselves from the society. Even the *saṁnyāsī*s or *avadhūta*s of this *dharma* are not social recluse. They do not stay confined to their *gādī* or *muṭh* seeking their own self-realization. Except for the four months of rainy season, they constantly move from village to village spreading the message of love, equality and social well-being.

Samatā

Samatā between one and the other is a key concept of Mahimā Dhrama. The instructions of Mahimā Svāmī as far as *samatā* is concerned is reflected very clearly in the following lines of Bhīmā Bhoi's writings:

> *In the abode of* Alekha
> *Nobody is important or unimportant.*
> *Everybody is blessed equally.*[1]

Again:

> Alekha Brahman Yogeśvara
> *Does not entertain any hatred or malice,*
> *He always considers everybody as equal*
> *Without discriminating between one's sins or good deeds.*
> *He permeates everything and being in the creation.*[2]

Here we come across a wonderful conception of equality that not only encompasses society but the world as such. This is more than evident from the fact that the followers of Mahimā Dharma during their congregation and even during their morning and evening prayers chant:

> Let there be welfare of the world (*jagat*), and let there be welfare of the *bhaktas*.[3]

Therefore, Bhīmā Bhoi often uses the word *samacitta* (a heart that treats everybody as equal) and *samāna dr̥ṣṭi* (an eye that sees everybody as equal).

One may be tempted here to compare notes with Mahāyāna Buddhism, especially its tantric version. We come across the notion

---

[1] *Bhajanamālā*, I.9.

[2] *Śrutinṣedha Gītā*, I.

[3] *jagata maṅgala heu; bhagata maṅgala heu.*

of *samatā* for the first time in the philosophy of the great Mahāyāna teacher Aśvaghoṣa. He describes the reality as *thathatā* (suchness). This may be taken as a positive expression of *śūnyatā*. According to him when the seeker realizes the true nature of *tathatā* he becomes conscious of the absolute oneness of the universe. This realization of oneness with the universe is called *samatā*. Vajrayāna, a branch of Mahāyāna Buddhism, develops this idea of oneness with the universe or *samatā* in greater detail. Indrabhūti, the famous *siddha* and the king of Sambalaka of Odisha, elaborated this idea in his *Jñānasiddhi* in greater detail. He categorically states that all these notions about *pāpa* and *puṇya*, pure and impure are but relative in nature.[4] What ultimately matters is the sublimation of ego and inculcating a sense of *samatā*, i.e. the knowledge that there is no distinction between God and the universe. According to Vajrayāna the Ādi-Buddha is believed to have generated five kinds of knowledge. One of them is *samatā-jñāna*.[5] This type of knowledge implies a form of wisdom that enables one to develop equal vision towards all. I have already indicated earlier that Mahimā Dharma, being originally the product of the soil, adheres to a large extent to the culture of assimilation that was the landmark of Odishan *sant* philosophy. Odiya *sant* philosophy reflects a wonderful syncretism of both – the Brāhmanic traditions (including Advaita Vedānta) and non-Brāhmanic traditions that includes Mahāyāna Buddhism, especially its tantric branches, and also Nātha Dharma. So this philosophical tradition encompasses within its fold many seminal ideas from divergent traditions. Though the Odia *sant*s were self-acclaimed Vaiṣṇavas, with an unprecedented zeal they accommodated within their metaphysical scheme many innovative ideas like God as *śūnya*, identity between *piṇḍa* and *brahmāṇḍa*, *jñāna-bhakti*, non-idolatry, dismissal of the *varṇa*-based hierarchy, and *samatā*. These theories do not have their roots exactly in the Brāhmanical religio-philosophical tradition. Some of the ideas

[4] Indrabhūti, *Jñānasiddhi*, X.34.

[5] Referred in F.D. Lessing and A.Wayman, *Introduction to Buddhist Tantric System*, p. 220.

are taken from the diverse forms of Buddhism that had left their footmarks on the land; and some of them reflect the theories of Nātha Dharma. Mahimā Dharma, though it emerged in Odisha some hundred years after the gradual recede of Utkalīya Vaiṣṇavism into oblivion, sprang up with unprecedented vigour. It cannot be denied that this *dharma* is a continuation of the tradition with some new and radical ideas. So there is no wonder that some of its principles reflect the Buddhist influences. Mahimā conception of *samatā* envisions equality of human beings between people and the universe as a whole. Though Utkalīya Vaiṣṇavas talked of *samatā* in this sense, the concept of *samatā* is more pronounced in Mahimā Dharma as we can gather from Bhīmā Bhoi's compositions. He writes:

Be they wicked or saintly,
Servant or master,
Insect or bird,
I see you equally in all beings,
Nowhere less than in another.

Who is present in earth, in stones, in wood,
in every lifeless thing?
My intellect knows only that there is only one
The one known as Śabda-Brahman.[6]

I an ignorant poet
Because of your compassion
I see all things as equal,
I cannot discriminate.
Satya Dharma is my witness.

Every creature of the three worlds
Has a different name, its own identity
Yet I know all of them have the same soul,
I make no distinction among them.[7]

---

[6] The indescribable *Brahman* that transcends the limits of language, yet it is the very principle of language/word, i.e. *śabda*.

[7] *Stuti-Cintāmaṇi*, 27th *bolī*.

This all-encompassing view of equality is unique in more than one sense. Many scholars prefer to call such an ideal a form of humanism. But can Bhīmā Bhoi's conception of *samatā* be adjusted within the narrow confines of humanism? The theory of humanism as such has more than one dimension; and very frankly speaking, umpteen numbers of definition of this word are likely to confuse one. Still very broadly speaking it can be said:

> Humanism is a philosophical and ethical stance that emphasizes the value or agency of human beings, individually and collectively, and generally prefers critical thinking and evidence (rationalism, empiricism) over established doctrine or faith (fideism).[8]

Humanism is based on the basic motto that humans are at the centre. The human is an end in itself. So in this scheme of thought what finally matters is human life and its dignity. Here one is not bound by the bond of equality with the nature. Nature lies at the periphery having an instrumental value for the mankind. Nature is the "other" having no intrinsic value of its own. Of course, we come across a very recent form of humanism called "inclusive humanism". It increasingly designates inclusive sensitivity to our species, planet and lives. But this inclusiveness finally aims at broadening of one's powers and obligations to the planet and the cosmos. Still we notice that a demarcating line between the people and nature perists. In this case human being is perceived as an agency that decides the policies on nature as a part of its *power*. Ultimately the human is placed in the centre. It is anthropocentric. But the Indian philosophical and ethical tradition is largely cosmo-centric. While discussing the nature of the cosmos it offers equal value to non-human beings and nature. It is based on the Upaniṣadic principle of "All is One; and One is All". In the case of Mahimā Dharma we notice the practical applicability of this Upaniṣadic principle. A truly realized soul can declare with ease: "Everybody is mine and I am yours".[9] For this *dharma* each aspect of creation has its own

---

[8] En.wikipedia.org

[9] *Bhajanamālā*, II.201.

value and identity, as is obvious from the verses quoted above. Yet all these diversities between the mobile and immobile, a piece of stone or a man, are finally bound by the principle "One is All; and All is One". So there should not be any hesitation in holding that they are of equal value. Even the label "spiritual humanism" does seem to be an appropriate designation for the inclusiveness that is displayed by Mahimā Dharma. The reason may be obvious. Humanism, at any cost, holds reason and evidence as its basis. But Mahimā philosophy emphasizes on transcending the limits of reason and believes that intuition or direct knowledge is the chief source of realization of unity amidst diversity. Its path is that of *a-sādhanā mārga*. Though Mahimā Dharma is not theistic in the general sense of the term it admits the transcendentality of *Śūnya-Brahman*. It believes in the path of *niṣkāma-bhakti* that implies surrendering the sense of personhood. All these presuppositions do not conform to the basic presupposition of humanism in general. Humanism seems to be too narrow a term to be applied to the Mahimā philosophy. We may call it a form of universalism that is all-inclusive. What is more remarkable in case of Mahimā Dharma, especially the way Bhīmā Bhoi presents it, is the unlimited concern for all the realms of the universe. Here the universality of equality turns into the universality of love and compassion (*karuṇā*). The concern flows as if from the heart, not from the intellect. One can feel the intensity of compassion from the following lines of Bhīmā Bhoi:

O Beginningless, indescribable One!
Save the ninefold earth[10] *and the three worlds*
O Lord save the human world
Young, old, children, male and female.

Birds, insects and creatures in the waters,
In whatever form you created them.
Grass and trees,
Mobile and immobile things,

[10] *Navakhaṇḍa*, a frequent division of world referred to in *Atharvaveda*, XI.7.14. Three earths are mentioned in *Atharvaveda*, VI.21.1.

Save the living beings who surrender.

xx xx xx

Give them deliverance by your name,
And be merciful to the sun and the moon
And to the countless (nine lakh) stars.[11]

Bhīmā Bhoi here displays the true character of a *sant*. We can draw a basic line of difference between a *bhakta* and a *sant*. A *bhakta* can afford to be selfish and individualistic in seeking *mukti* for himself, but a *sant* cannot afford to be selfish. God-realization for Mahimā Dharma is expanding oneself at the level of consciousness and tearing down the wall between people and the universe. A *sant* is one who suffers the pain of the suffering humanity.

Karuṇā

Once *samatā* between God, man and creation is deeply understood it naturally results in a form of compassion. One typical feature that marks the writings of Bhīmā Bhoi apart from the *sants* of his genre is his immense compassion for the humanity. It is a fact that the *sants* of the medieval era, including the Utkalīya Vaiṣṇavas, were concerned about the society and the injustice carried on in it in the name of religion. But Bhīmā Bhoi's concern for the society and the suffering humanity comes as if from the deep recesses of a sensitive heart. Degeneration of values and corrupt social practices deeply move him. His frustration and anger stem from this concern. He faithfully admits:

I suffer every pang as the sorrows
And sufferings of all beings pierce my heart.[12]

He was unable to bear the decadence and the evil ways the society in general resorted during his time. Bhīmā Bhoi ascribed it to the evil ways of Kaliyuga. So he fervently wished for the salvation for one and all. This deep feeling finds expression through different

---

[11] *Bhajanamālā*, I.17, translation taken from *Verses from the Void.*

[12] *Stuti-Cintamani*, 26th *bolī*, translation taken from *Verses from the Void.*

emotions. Sometimes he thinks that the entire cosmos would disintegrate due to wickedness and lack of *dharma*. Again, sometimes he wished for the new dawn, i.e. the era of *Satya*.

The day is ended, my work as well – what more to say?
Hoping for a better tomorrow.
I pass my days in this world,
Like this, the age comes to an end.[13]

Sometimes he feels the burden of sins and vices committed by the people are his own.

I neither have courage nor hope,
Tell me what to do.
Bear your own burden! Protect your devotees,
Take care of the world.

xx *xx* *xx*

Both fortune and calamity,
Both salvation and suffering are created by you.
Who will bear the burden of your sin and sorrow?
Let them lie at your feet.[14]

Sometimes he cries out to the Almighty:

A bone or two
A drop of blood, and a lump of flesh –
I carry such a frame
Mortal and frail.
How will I
Then not grieve over
The ceaseless sorrow
Of all living beings!

Endless are the agonies and sorrows of living
Who can bear to witness?
Condemn my life to hell

---

[13] *Stuti-Cintāmaṇi*, 50th *bolī*, translation taken from *Verses from the Void*.

[14] *Stuti-Cintāmaṇi*, 27th *bolī*.

But let the world be redeemed.[15]

The last two verses perfectly reflect the extent of his compassion. This may remind us of the Buddhist ideal of *karuṇā*. The concept is one of the most valuable contribution of Mahāyāna Buddhism. This concept is based on the altruistic interpretation of the concept of *nirvāṇa*. The Buddha had advised his followers to seek *nirvāṇa* for themselves. But for the Mahāyānīs personal liberation is not the goal; it is the liberation for the whole humanity. *Sūtrālaṁkāra*, the famous Buddhist text, very succinctly puts the ideal in the following lines:

> There is no *puṇya* if you feed yourself, but when you feed others; similarly, there is no greatness in personal liberation, it must be liberation for one and all.[16]

This compassionate identity with whole humanity lying in the vortex of misery and suffering is called *karuṇā*. The Mahāyānī ideal of *karuṇā* is encapsulated in the example of Avalokiteśvara, the compassionate one, who refused his personal *nirvāṇa*, until the worldly creatures could obtain freedom from suffering.

We note similar concern of Bhīmā Bhoi for the suffering of humanity. Suffering and human predicament in any form arouse compassion within his heart. The following lines bear witness to the exent of his sensitivity:

In the Mahābhārata war, five to ten heads roll
From a single stroke of a sword.
If you kick one limb
My other limb feels the pain.[17]

---

[15] *Stuti-Cintāmaṇi*, 27.19

[16] *Sūtrālaṁkāra*, VII.72.

[17] *Stuti-Cintāmaṇi*, 27th *bolī*.

Epilogue

So far I have highlighted the Mahimā theory of God as *śūnya* and the theoretical and practical corollaries that follow from this central presupposition. I have avoided any discussion on personal life of Bhīmā Bhoi and also on the institutionalized aspect of Mahimā Dharma. But I shall fail in my duties if I do not point out two paradoxes connected with Bhīmā Bhoi's life that to a great extent minimize his grand contributions to the popularity of Mahimā philosophy.

Bhīmā Bhoi: A Poet or a Philosopher?

Bhīmā Bhoi represented the true philosophy of Mahimā Dharma that not only inspired the followers of this order of faith but every common man. His explanation of very rarefied concepts like *Śūnya-Brahman/Puruṣa, niṣkāma-bhakti* and *ātma-jñāna* comes out with a rare type of lucidity. So it is unfortunate that Bhīmā Bhoi is portrayed by the modern scholars more as a poet than a philosopher. Open any web-portal on Bhīmā Bhoi, the only identity we come across is that of a poet. Bhīmā Bhoi definitely is a poet of the first order in Odia language. His choice of words, metaphors, unique lyricism and the depth of his emotion put him in the higher pedestal as a poet. This is evident from his heart-wrenching couplet:

> *Who can be a witness to all the sufferings of the humanity?*
> *Let me suffer in hell, but let the world be redeemed.*[1]

This couplet adorns the hall of the Indian parliament along with

[1] *prāṇiṅka ārtata duḥkha aparamita dekhu dekhu kebā sahu* ।
mo jībana pachhe narke padithāu jagata uddhar heu ॥
– *Stuti-Cintāmaṇi*, 27th *bolī*

the selected experts from other accredited regional languages. This proves his standing among Odia literati. Such was his poetic genius that it is believed he used to compose four *bhajana*s at a time and dictate them to four scribes: Hari Panda, Basu Panda, Markanda Dāsa and Dharmananda Dāsa. The first two scribes were brāhmaṇas and were provided by Guru Mahimā Svāmī. The two others joined him later. Such powerful outpouring of prolific poetry is unheard of in the history of literature. So there is no scope for doubt about Bhīmā Bhoi's poetic brilliance. But is not his philosophical innovativeness lost in the din of his fame as a poet? Most probably the impression is created from his hugely admired book *Stuti-Cintāmaṇi*. It is popular among the mass and elite alike. If cheap editions of this book are found with the street-corner shopkeepers, at the same time more than one version of its English translations (latest being *Verses from the Void* published in 2010) are available in the market. This work to some extent is autobiographical in nature. So most often he gets personal. He narrates his own sufferings as well as the suffering of the humanity, he pleads with the Almighty to come to the rescue; he narrates, complains, warns and sometimes gets highly frustrated by the injustice witnessed in the society. This phenomenon might have played an important role in creating the impression that Bhīmā Bhoi is just a literary genius. Readers and scholars pay little attention to his metaphysically-oriented treatises like *Brahma-Nirūpaṇa Gītā*, *Śrutiniṣedha Gītā* and *Nirveda Sādhanā* .These works discuss Mahimā views on the nature of *Śūnya-Brahman*, cosmology, soteriology and *bhakti*. Reviewers and critics very rarely take up such treatises for discussion. This might have been one of the possible reasons for labelling Bhīmā Bhoi exclusively as a poet. Finally, it appears that the scholars are so enamoured by his poetic power that they very rarely take note of the philosophical contents of his compositions including the *bhajana*s that are very often outrightly metaphysical in nature.

Despite his poetic talent we would be doing a great injustice to Bhīmā Bhoi if his philosophical acumen is not highlighted. I have already stated that his compositions have played a very crucial role in spreading the message of Mahimā during the initial phases of this movement. His *bhajana*s became an essential part of the Mahimā congregations with the sanction of Mahimā Svāmī. Even after the demise of the Master the practice continues. Thus the *bhajana*s somehow attained the status of the holy scripture of Mahimā Dharma from the middle of 1860s till 1930s. This is also a well-known fact that during this phase the adherent of this *dharma* were mostly drawn from the lower and downtrodden strata of the society having no access to the spiritual and philosophical theories. For them bare survival was more important than such luxuries of indulging in philosophical juggleries. Yet such people could be inspired by highly abstruse and sophisticated theories like *Śūnya-Brahman*, *Jīva-Brahman* identity, *piṇḍa–brahmāṇḍa* identity; this speaks volumes about Bhīmā Bhoi's capability of diving straight into the hearts of the people. Here I cite one such example of a very popular *bhajana* that so simply yet so profoundly expresses the basic idea about *Śūnya-Brahman*:

He roams in the temple of śūnya
The one without form and features.
Do not think of two feet[2]
Just cling to the one.

Indescribable city is his home.
O wise men, remember,
He is neither hot nor cold.

The flow of nectar, pure and untouched,
Unseen and unnamed,
Tastes sweet to the core.

Those who see him in the state of nirveda *(highest knowledge)*
Merge with the undivided Brahman.
They cross over birth and death.

Performing no rites or rituals
One finds him in the company of the wise.

---

[2] Most probably he was referring to dualism.

His initiation is niṣkāma dharma,
And his prayer is the one-lettered word.

In the presence of Brahman,
There is no rising or setting (eternal).
So says helpless Bhīmā,
the realm of transcendence (nigama)[3] *is impenetrable.*[4]

In these few couplets the entire range of the very concept of the Reality Supreme is elaborated. This is no small an achievement. The elites might stumble to understand the core meaning of such poems but for the common people (mostly from villages) who sing it lustily to the accompaniment of *khañjaṇī* (a type of percussion instrument) during evening congregations the implications of the verses are crystal clear. During my visit to the Khaliāpalī Āśrama of Bhīmā Bhoi I chanced to meet some Mahimā adherents and discussed with them about the ideas and ideals propagated by the philosopher. All of them were the illiterate people from the nearby villages. I was simply amazed by their depth of understanding of the central philosophy of Mahimā Dharma. They freely quoted from Bhīmā Bhoi's work to make their point.

In this book I have offered a detailed exposition of the philosophical depth of Mahimā Dharma as put forth in the writings of Bhīmā Bhoi. Despite the richness of his philosophical elucidation can we afford to be dogmatic and label him "just as a poet"? Should he be denied the right berth in the history of ideas just because he wrote his philosophical thought in the form of lyrical poetry? Does expressing philosophy in the lyrical form rob it off its philosophical content? I have already stated that since thirteenth century the very approach to doing philosophy had undergone a radical change. Philosophy was brought from the closed circle of the elites to the

---

3 According to R. Chainy, the compiler of *Sant (Sāhitya) Śabdakośa*, the dictionary of the words used in the *sant* literature, *nigama* means *a-mana*, i.e. the realm beyond ordinary categories of mind.

4 *Bhajanamālā*, I.8, translation taken from, *Verses from the Void* (ed. Bettina Bäumer). Necessary changes in certain words are mine.

commonest of the common. So the vernacular language and lyrical forms were chosen to reach out to these people. Most of them were illiterate. Lyrical poetry mostly composed in the form of songs could be appealing to such people; and they could easily remember them. Thus writing in the form of poetry does not make a philosopher a "just a poet". It is unfortunate that some academic philosophers are still the prisoners of the dogma that Indian philosophical literature is confined to the highly Sanskritized Classical phase during which writing in the form of Kārikās and Bhāṣyas were in vogue. It is high time that we get rid of such misconstrued notions.

Bhīmā Bhoi: The Contested Status

In this work my avowed task has been to explicate the philosophical foundation of Mahimā Dharma. As I have made it clear in the Introduction of the book, my entire analysis of the fundamental concepts of Mahimā Dharma is based on the writings of Bhīmā Bhoi. My stand, therefore, is likely to be contested by an influential section of the Mahimā-panthīs who staunchly believe that Mahimā Dharma is not very different from the so-called Sanātana Hindu Dharma based on Vedas, Purāṇas and Śāstras following Biśvanātha Bābā's neo-interpretation. So it becomes mandatory for me to say a few words about the unfortunate developments of Mahimā Dharma after Mahimā Svāmī left his mortal coils. Casting out of Bhīmā Bhoi from the mainstream Mahimā order is a case in point.

We should not lose track of the fact that Mahimā Svāmī had no written work. He had exclusively entrusted Bhīmā Bhoi with the task of spreading the message of this new religio-philosophical movement. Since Bhīmā Bhoi's *bhajanas* were exclusively sung at the Mahimā congregation in the presence of the *guru* it became a part of its rituals till 1930s when Biśvanātha Bābā took over the charge of the Mahimā institution at Joranda. It must be mentioned that Bhīmā Bhoi, though initiated directly by the founder of the *dharma,* was not an ascetic of the order. He was a family man – a *gṛhī bhakta* (householder). This may be one of the reasons why the ascetics of Mahimā order tried to disown the importance of Bhīmā Bhoi, though his *bhajanas* till 1930s had received the status of a holy scripture. There might have been other reasons as well for the seclusion of Bhīmā Bhoi from the mainstream. His place of activity had always been the Western part of Odisha from where he hailed. Here Bhīmā Bhoi had already attained the status of a *sant* and a godman amongst his followers. This might have created a good amount of discontent amongst the ascetics at the main centre situated at Joranda. In 1887 Bhīmā Bhoi established his own *āśrama* at Khaliāpalī of Sonepur, where he breathed his last.

The third factor that might have contributed to the distancing was the issue over admitting women in the *āśrama*. Bhīmā Bhoi staunchly believed in the equal status of man and woman. So a woman mendicant could be a part of his *āśrama*, that is strictly prohibited at the Joranda *āśrama*.

Unfortunately, the Mahimā movement that is very much alive in Odisha today is no longer centralized and a unitary form of *dharma*. It has now become polycentric. Different centres have emerged at different points in time. It is well known that a *dharma* is likely to change with the demise of the founder. This is usually followed by conflicts. The best example I can cite is the case of Buddhism. With the death of the Lord Buddha, Buddhism went on subdividing itself till the original teachings of the Bauddha *dharma* was lost in oblivion. Buddhism that started as a rebellious alternative movement against the weaker points of Vedism later on happily accommodated all that Lord Buddha was critical of. Right from admission of idolatry, including the worship of an array of gods and goddesses to the emphasis on mysterious tantric rites have now become the characteristics of modern Buddhism. In the case of Mahimā Dharma, though the change is not drastic, things are no better. The Mahimā community, apart from the laity, was divided into two rival ascetic orders – *balkaladhārīs* and *kaupīnadhārīs* – after the demise of the Master in 1876. The *balkaladhārīs* are called so because the ascetics wear a piece of bark of *kumbhī* tree. The *kaupīnadhārīs* only wear a loin-cloth. The story that Mahimā Svāmī himself initiated his first disciple Govind Bābā by offering him the bark (*balkala*) created the impression that *balkaladhārī*s were of higher order. This led to a struggle for power and influence.

It goes without saying that *balkaladhārī*s considered themselves at the top of the hierarchy as wearing *balkala* was considered to be the sign of *siddhi*. But *kaupīnadhārī*s refuse to accept their inferior status. However, things took a turn for the worse when Biśvanātha Bābā joined the order sometime in 1925 and later on became the head of the Joranda *gādī*; he asserted the superiority of the *balkaladhārī·samāja*. He introduced a distinction between the *apara saṁnyāsī* (imperfect) and *para saṁnyāsī* (perfect). Naturally, the *kaupīnadhārī*s were treated as *apara saṁnyāsī*s. Thus the separation between the two groups was complete. The *kaupīnadhārī*s are not allowed to enter into the temple precincts and are treated as outcaste. This ongoing struggle for land and power reminds one of Mahimā Svāmī's unusual act of not staying at one place for a long time and the burning of the *tuṅgī* (small establishments) after he left that place. Being a great Godman he realized how landed property and permanent establishments could make even a *saṁnyāsī* lose his head. To add to this Biśvanātha Bābā's attempt to interpret Mahimā Dharma as a coherent doctrine that is in consonance with the orthodox and Brāhmanical Sanskritized tradition totally sidelined Bhīmā Bhoi's contribution in making the Mahimā Dharma a popular movement. As Beltz correctly observes:

> Bhīmā Bhoi's revolutionary and challenging positions are neutralized and annihilated. The peculiarity of Mahimā Dharma as a protest movement and the extraordinary creativity of Bhīmā Bhoi became less visible.[5]

The new approach to Mahimā Dharma as a form of orthodox Hinduism had made it highly popular amongst the elites. But in this new scheme of interpretation of the history of this *dharma*

---

[5] Johannez Beltz, 2007, "Contested Authorities, Disputed Centres, Rejected Norms: Situating Mahimā Dharma in Its Regional Diversity" in G. Pfeffer (ed.) *The Centre and the Periphery: Studies in Orissan History, Religion and Anthropology*, New Delhi: Manohar, p. 88.

Bhīmā Bhoi has no significant contribution. He is depicted just as a disciple of Mahimā Svāmī who could compose the lyrical poetry containing the essence of Mahimā Dharma only due to the vision bestowed upon him by the *guru*. Bhīmā Bhoi of course, out of sheer humility and his unflinching devotion to Mahimā Svāmī, often admitted his social background and attributed his poetic genius to the *guru*. But that does make him a cipher. But the way he is portrayed by Biśvanātha Bābā negates his contribution as an independent authority.

What is more interesting is that besides the question of power and property, the status of Bhīmā Bhoi is a point of reference in the ongoing fight of influence among the two groups. There seems to be a different perception of Bhīmā Bhoi: while the *kaupīnadhārī*s claim to follow Bhīmā Bhoi's books as the holy book, the *balkaladhārī*s seem to take Bhīmā Bhoi as one amongst the other. Speaking for the *balkaladhārī* community Biśvanātha Bābā said that the books of Bhīmā Bhoi are not taken as the books laying down the regulations and rules of conduct; since they are accepted as religious books, they are read along with others.[6]

From the researches conducted by A. Eschmann, Johannes Beltz and others it appears that the causes for the division between two groups are not as simple as they appear. Social hierarchy plays an important role here. It is found that the *kaupīnadhārī*s are predominant in the western part of Odisha, the members of which are largely drawn from the former untouchables called *ganda pana*s. On the other hand, the *balkaladhārī*s are more prominent in Joranda and central Odisha with most of its followers drawn from the comparatively rich, educated and upper-caste people like farmers.

But my aim in no way is to delve into the story of sectarianism and power game. My objective is to throw light on the hitherto neglected philosophy of Mahimā Dharma as projected in its initial

---

6 Deposition of Avadhuta Bisvanatha Baba before the Endowment Commission, Cuttack, 28 March 1961, South Asia Institute, Orissa Archive, MSS, 175.

stages by Bhīmā Bhoi. That he preached the basics of Mahimā Dharma through popular poetry has not been denied even by his worst critic within the mainstream Mahimā circle. Till date the *bhajanas* composed by him are an essential part of the daily ritual at Joranda Mahimā *gādī*.[7]

I referred to the turn of events in the Mahimā movement simply to highlight what I had been saying repeatedly. India has always witnessed the emergence of reformatory movements from time to time. But the power of orthodoxy has been so strong that the voice of dissent had always been subdued in the din of our so-called Sanātana Dharma.

Fortunately for us, Mahimā Dharma, as it exists in different forms in different parts of Odisha, has not yet lost all the ideals it once stood for. The followers continue to be non-idolators; they still live a simple life and follow the moral codes prescribed by the founder. They continue to chant *Alekha Mahimā* under the open sky facing the sun; they continue to believe in the supremacy of *Śūnya-Brahman*. Above all, the people of rural Odisha still love to sing the *bhajanas* of Bhīmā Bhoi, whether they follow his *dharma* or not. His works continue to rule the heart of at least, the rural and common folk of Odisha.

---

[7] Johanennes Beltz records that during an interview with a *balkaladhārī bābā* at Joranda *āśrama* he told, "We certainly like Bhīmā Bhoi's writings because his words are inspired by Mahimā Svāmī. But he was a tribal and illiterate. What Mahimā Svāmī told him he wrote." – "Introduction: Bhīmā Bhoi: Life and Legends", *Bhīmā Bhoi: Verses from the Void*.

APPENDIX

Mahimā Dharma
Buddhism or Classical Advaitism?

FROM our discussion it is clear that the use of the word *śūnya* does not make Mahimā Dharma an offshoot of Śūnyavāda, nor the use of the word *Brahman* turn Mahimā Dharma into a replication of Advaita. Yet the Mahimā scholars inclined either to this side or the other side of the traditional divide between Buddhism and Brāhmanism are in search for its genesis this way or that way. A serious look at the materials available on Mahimā philosophy reveals that the chain of action and reaction started with N.N. Vasu's interpretation of Mahimā Dharma as a form of Buddhism. The first reaction perhaps comes from the *siddha* of the Mahimā order – Biśvanātha Bābā. In order to prove that Mahimā Dharma is not a form of "New Buddhism" he goes to the other extreme to prove that it is very much a part of the orthodox Brāhmanical tradition. He attaches a new label to its philosophical position, viz. Viśuddhādvaitism. The followers of a section of Mahimā-panthīs take Bābā's interpretation as final and sacrosanct. I shall devote the following pages to these two distinct positions as far as Mahimā philosophy is concerned.

Is Mahimā Dharma a Form of Buddhism?

N.N. Vasu was the first scholar to be fascinated by this indigenous philosophical trend of Odisha. Full credit must be given to him for bringing this to the notice of the intelligentsia that such a unique system of thought existed in the land. He designates Mahimā Dharma as New Buddhism. But the word "Buddhism" itself is nebulous. Here the term "Buddhism" should be understood with little more caution. "Buddhism" as such does not refer to a uniform set of philosophical presuppositions. Buddhism in the later phases branched off to many schools and sub-schools with divergent philosophical foundations, viz. Sthaviravāda, Mādhyamika, Vijñānavāda, Yogācāra, Sautrāntika, to name a few. Each one of these sub-systems held differing positions regarding the nature of Reality. So we must first of all understand what does Vasu mean by Buddhism? As the title of the book, *Modern Buddhism and Its Followers in Odisha*, suggests, he was primarily referring to the tantric forms of Buddhism, especially Vajrayāna that had a strong presence in Odisha till the end of seventeenth century CE. This school of thought modified the basic principles of various branches of Mahāyāna and combined it with the philosophy of Tantra. Vajrayāna retained the Mādhyamika conception of the indescribable and ineffable principle of *śūnyatā* as the focal point of its philosophy and theism. So Vasu built his thesis on two terms profusely used in the *sant* literature of Odisha, especially in the works of Pañcasakhā, viz. *śūnya* and Buddha. Since tantric form of Buddhism was widespread in Odisha from seventh century CE to seventeenth century CE he argues that the Odia *sant*s of sixteenth century CE were Buddhist in spirit though they concealed their true affiliation and claimed themselves to be Vaiṣṇavas. It is a fact that the Vaiṣṇavas of Odisha, including the five famous poets, delineated the Highest Reality as *Śūnya-Puruṣa* or *Brahman*. Similarly, these *sant*s of Odisha for generations have used the word "Buddha" as an epithet for Jagannātha, the Vaiṣṇava deity of Odisha. It is also a fact that some of them were prosecuted by the king of Odisha for holding on to such unusual religious view.

There are definitely some grains of truth in Vasu's analysis. But on the basis of this presumption he comes to the abrupt conclusion that *sant*s of Odisha were "Crypto Buddhists" who concealed their true affiliation for the fear of social and royal ostracization. But when he scans Mahimā Dharma in the last chapter of his book he falters and tries to fit Mahimā Dharma almost forcibly to support his thesis. He not only misplaces the facts about Mahimā Svāmī and Bhīmā Bhoi but provides some baseless arguments to prove that Mahimā Dharma is "New Buddhism". Let us examine here some of his arguments to judge their viability.

First, Vasu states that the Buddhists never designated their faith as "Buddhism", rather they are found to call it *sadharma* or *sad-dharma*. Then he goes on to argue:

> Following this the Utkala community of Buddhists has given the name "Mahimā Dharma" to its creed and styles itself as Mahimā-dharmin.[1]

Finally he concludes:

> Under the benign spirit of religious toleration and the noble and fostering spirit of freedom of thought inaugurated and scrupulously adhered to by the British government, this community has began, for forty years to rouse itself up, to throw its masks and to reassert duly.[2]

But Vasu should have remembered that the word *dharma* is not the exclusive preserve of the Buddhists. The term was used by the orthodox systems of thought quite frequently like "Bhāgavata Dharma" or "Śaiva Dharma". So the use of the word *dharma* by no stretch of imagination makes the Mahimā system of thought a form of Buddhism. Second, Vasu compliments the British attitude of tolerance towards non-Semitic religion that had helped the followers of Mahimā Dharma to come out in the open and preach the New Buddhism. But all the reports prepared under the aegis of the British government nowhere mentions that Mahimā Dharma is a form of Buddhism. I have already discussed the social and cultural compulsions that led to the rise and popularity of this new *dharma*. Even the worst orthodox critics of Mahimā Dharma would not brand it as Buddhism. So the entire argument of Vasu is based on unfounded conjectures.

Again Vasu presents another conjecture to prove the Buddhistic lineage of Mahimā Dharma. In this case he refers to the Mahimā pattern of worship as *Alekha Para-Brahman* under the open sky twice a day facing the sun. He relates this practice to Hīnayāna Buddhism.

---

[1] Vasu, *Modern Buddhism and Its Followers*, p. 150.

[2] Ibid., p. 151.

He observes:

> . . . as a sequel to the worship of the sun and fire into primitive Buddhist society, the Hīnayānists have not been able to throw off these deities altogether, though they have done away with the worship of others. Yet it is interesting to note that in the *Yaśomatī Mālikā* of the Mahimā-dharmīs, lingering traces of this faith are to be met with. And just as the Buddhists of the middle ages regarded Buddha or Bodhisattva as the Devātideva, i.e. God of gods, the Mahimā-dharmīs also look up to Jagannātha or Buddha as being the greatest and Supreme object of worship.[3]

In this case the argument is full of inconsistencies. Earlier he had highlighted on the word *Śūnya*, a Mahāyānic concept to prove the Buddhistic affiliation of the Mahimā-dharmīs. Now from nowhere he brings in Hīnayāna and its practice of worshipping the sun as the primary link between Buddhism and Mahimā Dharma. Then he again reverts back to Mahāyāna practice of worshipping Buddha and *bodhisattva*s (the Hīnayānists never worshipped Buddha) to show that Mahimā-dharmīs also worship Buddha or Jagannātha. In fact, Mahimā-dharmīs neither worship Buddha nor Jagannātha. As already discussed they are non-idolators. The entire argument is muddled and confusing. We fail to know whether the Mahimā Dharma is an offshoot of Mahāyāna or Hīnayāna. Besides, there is no place for the worship of Buddha or Jagannātha in the Mahimā scheme of religion as Vasu claims. Vasu's argument as far as Mahimā Dharma is concerned is most often based on wild conjectures. So he utterly fails to prove that Mahimā Dharma is New Buddhism. It now becomes obvious that the followers of this *dharma* react so sharply to Vasu's interpretation.

However to be academically honest we must thank Vasu for bringing into light certain issues that cannot be brusquely set aside. First and foremost, the use of two terms *śūnya* and "Buddha" by the preceding *sant*s as well as by the Mahimā-panthīs needs to be probed. Not only Mahimā Dharma but the religious literature of Odisha

---

[3] Vasu, op. cit., p. 175.

use the term *śūnya* quite frequently. The concept of *Śūnya-Puruṣa/ Śūnya-Brahman* was not peculiar to Bhīmā Bhoi. Right from fifteenth century CE the concept plays an important role in Odia literature. Sant Sāralā Dāsa in his transcreation of *Mahābhārata* introduces the term without impunity. Surprisingly, the orthodox section of the society did not object to such use. Again, Vasu rightly hints at the unusual use of the term "Buddha" with reference to the Vaiṣṇavic deity like Jagannātha. In no other religious tradition a Vaiṣṇavic deity or for that matter any Hindu deity is so closely associated with Buddha. Vasu also very successfully brings to our notice the acquaintance of the Odia culture with the various sub-traditions of Buddhism. Right from Sāralā Dāsa in the fifteenth century CE to Bhīmā Bhoi of nineteenth century CE all refer to four branches of Buddhism — Nāgāntī, Yogāntī, Vedāntī and Siddhāntī. Such labels are atypical and one may not find such names in the history of Buddhism. Most probably they were the regional versions of Tantric Buddhism. Followers of Nāgārjunapāda, the great Buddhist tantric, were called "Nāgāntī", the followers of Yogācāra school were called "Yogāntī", the followers of Sautrāntika school were called "Vedāntī" and the Vajrayānīs were known as "Siddhāntī". These systems of thought were most probably the regionalized versions of Buddhism that flourished in Odisha. All these suggestions made by Vasu cannot be dismissed off hand.

Is Mahimā Dharma a Part of Sanātana Dharma?

I have already stated that Vasu's off-handish handling of Mahimā Dharma and his weak arguments to prove the Buddhist lineage of this *dharma* naturally led to a sharp reaction from the Mahimā-panthīs. The later *siddhas* of Mahimā order, especially those belonging to the *gādī* at Joranda, vehemently oppose this view. Biśvanātha Bābā, a renowned scholar of classical Indian tradition and virtually the non-disputed *saṁnyāsī* of this institution, took up the challenge to offer a systematic exposition of Mahimā Dharma. He was not only a great scholar but a prolific writer. As I have stated earlier, Mahimā Svāmī, the founder of this *dharma,* had no written work. He entrusted the task to Bhīmā Bhoi, who followed the santhic style of writing in the form of *bhajanas* and poetic treatises in simple vernacular language. It was Bhīmā Bhoi who was largely responsible for making the traits of this new *dharma* popular through his innumerable works. But he was no scholar. He wrote from his heart. So during the first half of twentieth century CE, Avadhūta Biśvanātha Bābā took up the task of providing a systematic exposition of Mahimā Dharma in his voluminous work *Sarvatattva Sāra Śiromaṇi Alekha Brahman Darśanam*. As the title of the work suggests he scans through varied *tattvas*, including Vedas, Upaniṣads, Smṛtis like *Manu Saṁhitā* and Purāṇas, and even tantric literature to prove that Mahimā Dharma is out and out a form of Advaitism of the Vedāntic Order.

As I have pointed out in the introductory chapter, essentially there is not much of a discrepancy between Bhīmā Bhoi's delineation of Mahimā philosophy and Biśvanātha Bābā's version of it. Both admitted that the Reality Supreme is One and unique that eludes conceptualization and determination. Both hold that the reality is non-scriptable and ineffable Absolute *Brahman*. Both subscribed to the theory of *jñāna-bhakti*. Both believed in non-idolatry and the futility of rites and rituals. But Bhīmā Bhoi never consciously made any effort to systematically present the faith. He wrote from his heart and that appealed to the commonest of the common; on the other hand Biśvanātha Bābā was a scholar and intellectual who was guided by the strong motivation to set the records straight. He was bent upon proving that Mahimā Dharma is not a dissident movement but a part of the Sanātana Dharma based on Śāstras sanctioned by the Brāhmanical tradition. Biśvanātha Bābā's works try to place the Mahimā philosophy in the classical and Sanskritized philosophical setting. He quotes profusely from all the Śāstras available in orthodox tradition in support of each of the principles valued by Mahimā Dharma. In the process he uproots a very novel and indigenous philosophy from its local settings and posts it in the midst of varied and sometimes conflicting systems of classical tradition. He takes the help of selective Sanskrit verses without any reference to the context and in the process sometimes goes against the very original flavour of this *dharma*. One might not have any problem in accepting his thesis that Mahimā Dharma is a form of Viśuddhādvaitavāda, for, it centres on a pure form of non-dualism that defies the discrimination between God and the world on the one hand, and God and the individual self on the other. In innumerable verses Bhīmā Bhoi narrated this. But this could have been done without the support of the variegated Śāstras that most often are not complimentary. This view has been supported by most of the modern scholars including Eschmann,[4] Bäumer,[5] Siddhartha Das,[6] Nepak[7] and others. In the process of claiming it to be a part of Sanātana Dharma he robs it off its novelty.

Moreover, to prove the orthodox affiliation of the *dharma* Biśvanātha Bābā emphasizes more on the term *Brahman* than the word *śūnya*. Thereby, he tried to prove that the *dharma* has nothing to do with Buddhism. In this work he remains absolutely non-committal about the use of the word – *śūnya* and "Buddha" that were so frequently used by Bhīmā Bhoi. It appears somehow amazing that the *bhajana*s of Bhīmā Bhoi containing the word *sūnya*, that were mostly composed during the lifetime of Mahimā Svāmī, and are sung in the Mahimā *gādī* like Joranda could now be relegated to the oblivion. Biśvanātha Bābā makes a brief reference to the

[4] A. Eschmann points out that Biśvanātha Bābā quotes from varied orthodox texts that sometimes are contradictory. "Mahimā Dharma: An Autochthonous Hindu Reform Movement", in A. Eschmann et al. (eds.) *The Cult of Jagannath and the Regional Tradition of Orissa*.

[5] Bettina Bäumer: "It is thus more surprising that the *dharma* has been completely Vedānticized by Biśvanātha Bābā, an interpretation which not only goes against Bhīmā Bhoi's thought, but against the whole tenet of Mahimā Dharma", "Introduction", in Bettina Bäumer and J. Beltz (eds.) *Bhīmā Bhoi: Verses from the Void*.

[6] Siddhartha Das: ". . . the texts of Bābā undermine the spirit and essence of the original ideas of the sect. By Sanskritizing its ideas, Bābā has done a great dis-service to the purpose of the sect, whose base lies among the rural illiterate mass", *Mahimā Dharma: A Cultural Dissent*, Cuttack: Arya Prakashan, 1997, p. 53.

[7] Nepak 1972.

word with the off-handish comment that *śūnya* is not exclusively a concept of Buddhist origin. We entirely agree with him. But he quotes mostly from some later Upaniṣads in support of his thesis without ever unfolding whether such use was there in orthodox philosophical tradition before the Mahāyāna Buddhists came out with their theory of *śūnya*. In fact, he prefers to remain totally silent about the *śūnya*-centric metaphysical tradition of Odisha, preferring to rely heavily on the holy scriptures of the Brāhmanical tradition. A man with in-depth knowledge of the intellectual tradition of India could have dealt with the issue more adequately. He was fully aware that the word *śūnya* does not mean "absence" but non-conceptualizability, as is evident from his analysis of a verse from *Yogavāsiṣṭha Rāmāyaṇa*. But he refuses to take up for discussion Nāgārjuna's concept of *śūnyatā* and his conception of the non-duality (*advyaya*) due to inexplicable reasons. What surprises us more is his handling of Buddhist philosophy. He never directly hits at the Mahāyāna conception of *śūnyatā* and *tathatā*, instead digresses to refute the Buddhist (Yogācāra and Mādhyamika) cosmology. As a great scholar he must have been associated with the Vajrayāna texts like *Jñānasiddhi* and *Advayavajra Saṁgraha*. Both the works include within its metaphysical fold the concept of *ātman*, as opposed to the original Buddhist trend. Both the works admit that the highest reality is the potential womb (*śūnyatā-garbha*) of the cosmic process that is so akin to Biśvanātha Bābā's interpretation of the Mahimā cosmology. Both the works accommodate the concept of God within the scheme of an ineffable and indescribable reality. We note the dismissive attitude regarding the frequent use of Buddha in Mahimā literature. As a child of the colloquial Odia culture he should have known that it was not only Bhīmā Bhoi, but a series of Odia *sant*s since fifteenth century CE, who have eulogized the Buddha. They have identified the Buddha with the Reality Supreme. But Bābā skilfully winds up the issue by an etymological analysis of the word Buddha, i.e. the word has been derived from the root *budh* signifying "enlightenment" and "knowledge", turning a blind eye to its profuse use with reference to God in the Odia tradition. Such use had become the benchmark of Odia philosophical tradition.

In his zeal to prove the Brāhmanic origin of Mahimā Dharma, he avoids every concept and idea remotely connected with Buddhism. But he prefers to remain silent on the issue as the affiliation to Sanātana Dharma seems to be academically and religiously much more lucrative to the intellectuals to whom the book was addressed.

Finally, what is likely to surprise innumerable admirers of this unparalleled *dharma* is the way Biśvanātha Bābā contradicts some of the basic values championed by Mahimā Svāmī. It is well known that Mahimā Dharma eschews some of basic presuppositions of Sanātana Dharma, viz. caste discrimination, meaningless rituals (*saṁskāras*) and the unquestionable authority of the Śāstras. But in his eagerness to give this *dharma* orthodox identity he throws all caution to the wind. He even goes to the extent of supporting the oppressive caste system by quoting some lines from *Mahābhārata* (Anuśāsana-Parva) that instructs "Never accept food from a śūdra. O Devī! this has been always taken as forbidden food by the gods." While elaborating the *śloka* further Bābā takes the help from the *Gītā* that states "the inherent *svadharma* of the śūdra is to serve the members of the higher caste".[8] This is in a sense shocking, for, the favourite motto of Mahimā Dharma is:

> *jāti khojile mukti nāhi, mukti khojile jāti nāhi*
>
> If you search for *jāti* (caste) then forget about *mukti*;
> and if you are desirous of *mukti* then do not bother about *jāti.*

Such explications go against the historical compulsions that made the socially oppressed see a ray of hope in Mahimā Dharma. Equality of mankind is one of the benchmarks of this *dharma*. So Bhīmā Bhoi reiterates:

> *When all became outcastes*
> *He (Mahimā Svāmī) appeared as the mighty Lord*
> *To turn devotees to one caste.*[9]

---

[8] Biśvanātha Bābā, 1998, *Sarva Vedavedānta Śiromaṇi Alekha Para-Brahman Darśanam*, part I, Cuttack: Mahimā Dharmalocana Parisad, p. 619.

[9] *Bhajanamālā*, II.14.

Astonishingly enough, Biśvanātha Bābā himself shares the same view in his poetic work *Cinmaya Brahma-Gītā*. Herein he declares:

> *There is no place for caste distinction in Brahman-bhakti*
> *Do not discriminate between the high and the low.*[10]

So it appears completely jarring when Biśvanātha Bābā quotes from the typically rites and ritual-based treatises to prove the orthodox affiliation of Mahimā Dharma. For example, *Manu Saṁhitā* not only champions rigid discrimination of the mankind on the basis of caste, but also ordains the strict adherence to rituals or *saṁskāras*. Again, he takes the help of such Smr̥ti texts as *Bhāgavata Purāṇa* and *Vāyu Purāṇa*. Both the works, though of high philosophical content, champion the worship of idols and personal deities. *Bhāgavata Purāṇa* speaks of *navadhā-bhakti* that includes worship of the idols (*arcana*). Biśvanātha Bābā does not even mind quoting from the tantric texts like *Rudra-Yāmala* that also deals with the practice of tantric rituals. If we are to rely on Bhīmā Bhoi's version of Mahimā Dharma then it becomes clear that this *dharma* did not have much to do even with Vedas, the most sacred reference point of the Sanātana Dharma. So he suggests the path of *nirveda*, i.e. the path that transcends Veda. I think Mahimā Svāmī, the founder of the *dharma*, would not have disapproved of this for such lines appear in his collection of *bhajanas* that has received the unanimous approval of the Mahimā-panthīs of all denominations.

We must realize that in Indian tradition the term *dharma* understood as religion is never confined within the strict boundaries of a definite set of principles and faiths. It has always accommodated the voice of dissent. Not only Mahimā Dharma but many such religious sects including the Śaiva-Siddhānta, Kashmir Śaivism and Nātha Dharma defied Śruti and Smr̥ti. But they are never considered as outsiders or *nāstikas*. It is a fact that Mahimā Dharma has never been seen as a form of *nāstika dharma*, but always a part of the wide spectrum of Hindu Dharma, despite its anti-Brāhmanical tone and tenor. So Biśvanātha Bābā's interpretation might have quelled the

---

[10] *Cinmaya Brahma-Gītā*, II canto.

ill-feelings of the staunch Sanātanavādins but in the process of such an interpretation he risks the very identity of Mahimā Dharma.

From our detailed discussion this is now amply proved that Mahimā philosophy is neither an offshoot of Buddhism nor a subsidiary of Vedism/Brāhmanism. The very concept of God as *Śūnya-Brahman*, therefore, needs to be probed again to understand its genesis.

Mahimā Dharma: The Indegenous Product of the Soil

Now we come back to our initial question – Is Mahimā Dharma a form of Buddhism or a part of Sanātana Dharma based on Vedas, Upaniṣads, *Gītā* and *Bhāgavata*? We have already noted the alternative interpretations offered by N.N. Vasu and Biśvanātha Bābā; however, the true genesis of Mahimā Dharma remains unexplored. The ground for the rejection of both the interpretations is simple, yet often ignored. We must remember that Mahimā philosophy is not scholastic and academic in nature. It is a philosophy that was in fact translated into a way of life. I have already indicated that the new *dharma* had its base in the non-elite section of the populace. So how did these illiterate people immediately took to this way of life that discards idol worship, the observance of traditional rituals and *saṁskāra*s? This has been the Hindu way of life for ages. How could such common and illiterate people so quickly adopt to a totally distinct form of religion that preaches devotion to formless, indescribable, non-attributable, *Śūnya-Brahman*? This form of *dharma* seems too sophisticated for the common mass. The popularity of the Mahimā (especially Bhīmā Bhoi's *bhajana*s) in the remotest parts of Odisha, at least proves one thing. The common people of Odisha were already acquainted with the conception of God who could be formless, nameless, *śūnya* yet *Brahman*. Thus we may now come to the conclusion that Mahimā philosophy is but a continuation of the philosophico-culture that had become a part of Odishan life. Maybe, this *dharma* is more radical and more illuminative in nature, yet it is very much a part of this culture. This view is strongly suggested by such scholars as

Mahatab,[11] Mansingh,[12] Eschmann,[13] Nepak[14], Bäumer[15] and many others. All of them hold that Mahimā Dharma is a more illuminative and radical form of *sant* philosophy that was nurtured in Odisha through its association with divergent philosophical streams.

[11] Mahatab 1961.

[12] Mansingh 1982.

[13] Eschmann 1978.

[14] Nepak 1971.

[15] Bäumer 2010.

Bibliography

Original Sources (Odia Texts)

Bhīmā Bhoi, *Adyanta Gītā*.

———, *Aṣṭaka Bihārī-Gītā*.

———, *Bhajanamālā*.

———, *Brahma-Nirūpaṇa Gītā*.

———, *Cautīsa Madhucakra*.

———, *Mahimā Bhajana*.

———, *Nirveda Sādhanā*.

———, *Śrutiniṣedha Gītā*.

———, *Stuti-Cintāmaṇi*.

(All these books are published by Dharma Grantha Store, Cuttack, and they are undated)

———, 1950, *Stutichintamani*, ed. A.B. Mohanty, Bhubaneswar: Utkal University.

———, 1970, *Bhajanamālā*, ed. A.B. Mohanty, Bhubaneswar: Utkal University.

Biśvanātha Bābā, 1931, *Mahimā Dharma Pratipādaka*, Cuttak: Satya Mahimā Dharmalocana Samiti.

———, *Sarva Veda Vedānta Sāratattva Śiromaṇi, Alekha Paraman Brahman Darśanam*, vol. I, Cuttack: Mahimā Dharmalocana Samiti.

———, 2000, *Alekha Parama Brahma Darśanam, Sarva Veda Vedānta Sāratattva Śiromaṇi*, vol. II, Cuttack: Mahimā Dharmalocana Samiti.

———, 1971, *Mahimā Dharma Darśana Tattva*, Cuttack: Mahimā Dharmalocana Samiti.

Allied Sources (Odia Texts)

(All these books are published by Dharma Grantha Store, Cuttack)

Acyutānanda Dāsa, *Śūnya Saṁhitā.*

———, *Śūnya Saṁhitā, Causaṭhī Ṭikā.*

———, *Jñāna Pradīpa Gītā.*

———, *Cabisa Paṭala.*

———, *Śabda Brahma Saṁhitā.*

———, *Kaivarta Gītā.*

———, *Tattvabodhinī.*

———, *Caurāsī Yantra.*

Arakṣita Dāsa, *Mahimandal Gītā.*

Balarāma Dāsa, *Brahmāṇḍa Bhūgola.*

———, *Virāṭa Gītā.*

Caitanya Dāsa, *Nirguṇa Māhātmya.*

———, *Viṣṇugarbha Purāṇa.*

Dvārakā Dāsa, *Gupta Gītā.*

Jagannātha Dāsa, *Tuḷa Bhiṇā.*

———, *Bhāgavata.*

Secondary Sources

BOOKS (ODIA)

Chaini, R., 1994, *Oriyā Sant Sāhitya Śabdakosa*, Cuttack: Arya Prkashan.

Das, Cittaranjan, 1952, *Odishara Mahimā Dharma*, Bhubaneswar: Orissa Sahitya Akademi.

Dash, S., 1993, *Bhaktakavi Bhīmā Bhoi*, Cuttack: Navodaya Prakashana.

Mishra, Narasingha, 2007, *Śūnya Maṇḍapara Sant*, Cuttack: Cuttack Students Store.

Mohanty, B., 1965, *Odishara Nātha Dharma*, Cuttack: Friends Publishers.

Nath, S., 1990, *Mahimā Dharmadhārā*, Bhubaneswar: Hemalata Nath.

———, 1995, *Mahimā Dharma Prakāśa O Vikāsa*, Satya Mahimā Ashrama.

Nayak, Uddhava C., 1985, *Mahimā Dharma Viśva Itihāsa.*

Pradhan, N.N., 1986, *Prācīna Odiya Sāhityare Nirgunara Dhārā*, Cuttack:

Dharma Grantha Store.

Sahoo, K. (ed.), 1988, *Bhaktakavi Bhīmā Bhoi Granthāvalī*, Dharma Grantha Store.

Sarala Sahitya Sansad, 1997, *Sant Kabi Bhīmā Bhoi*, Cuttack: Odisha Book Store.

Swami Satyananda, 1988, *Mahimā Dharma*, Cuttack: Chandi Pustakalaya.

PAPERS (ODIA)

Kar, B., 1970-71, Mahimā Dharmara Eka Dārśanika Paryālocana", *Jhankara*, Cuttack.

Mishra, K.C., 1972, "Mahimā Dharma O Odiyā Sāhitya", in *Mahimā Dharma and Darśana*, ed. D. Panda, Koraput: D.A.V. College.

Panigrahi, K.C., 1972, "Bhīmā Bhoi", in *Mahimā Dharma and Darśana*, ed. D. Panda, Koraput: D.A.V. College.

Pradhan, N.N., 1972, "Mahimā O Odiya Sahitya", in *Mahimā Dharma and Darśana*, ed. D. Panda, Koraput: D.A.V. College.

BOOKS (ENGLISH)

Bäumer, B. and Johannes Beltz, 2010, *Bhīmā Bhoi: Verses from the Void: Mystic Poetry of an Odiya Saint*, New Delhi: Manohar.

Bäumer, B. and J.R. Dupuche, 2005, *Void and Fullness in Hindu, Buddhist and Christian Traditions, Śūnya-Pūrṇa-Plerôma*, New Delhi: D.K. Printworld.

Bhattacharyya, B., 1989, *An Introduction to Buddhist Esoterism*, Delhi: Motilal Banarsidass.

——— (ed.), 1929, *Two Vajrayani Works (Jñānasiddhi & Prajñopāya Viniścayasiddi)*, Baroda: Gaekwad Oriental Series.

Copley, A., 2003, *Hinduism in Public and Private: Reform, Hindutva, Gender, Sampradaya*, New Delhi: Oxford University Press.

Das, C.R., 1982, *A Glimpse into Odiya Litarature*, Bhubaneswar: Orissa Sahitya Akademi.

Das, Siddhartha, 1997, *Mahimā Dharma: A Cultural Dissent*, Arya Prakashan.

Dasgupta, S.B., 1974, *An Introdution to Tantric Buddhism*, Calcutta: University of Calcutta.

———, 1976, *Obscure Religious Cults*, Calcutta: Firma K.L.M.

———, 1991, *Devotional Poets and Mystics*, parts I & II, New Delhi: Ministry of Information and Broadcasting, Govt. of India.

Eschmann, A. et al., 1986, *Jagannath and the Regional Cults Orissa*, New Delhi: Manohar.

Hess, Linda and Sukhdev Singh, 2001, *The Bījak of Kabīr*, Delhi: Motilal Banarsidass.

Hiriyanna, M., 1994, *Outlines of Indian Philosophy*, Delhi: Motilal Banarsidass.

Kar, B., 1984, *Major Trends in Orissan Philosophy*, Cuttack: Grantha Mandir.

Krishna, Daya et al., 2002, *Bhakti: A Contemporary Discussion*, New Delhi: Indian Council of Philosophical Research.

Kulke, H. Schneppel, 2001, *Jagannath Revisited*, New Delhi: Munshiram Manoharlal.

Majumadar, B.C., 1911, *Sonepur in the Sambalpur Tract*, Brahmo Mission Press.

Mahapatra, S., 1983, *Bhīmā Bhoi*, New Delhi: Sahitya Akademi.

Mahatab, H.K., 1961, *History of Orissa*, Cuttack: Cuttack Students Store.

Mehrotra, A.K. (tr.), 2011, *Songs of Kabir*, New York: NYRB Classics, p. 29.

Mishra, K.C., 2000, *Studies in Mahimā Dharma*, Bhubaneswar: Institution of Orissan Culture.

Mukherjee, P., 1941, *History of Medieval Vaiṣṇavism in Orissa*, Calcutta.

Nātha, S., 1990, *Mahimā Dharmadhara*, Bhubaneswar.

Nepak, B., 1999, *Bhīmā Bhoi*, Bhubanwswar: Bhagiratha Prakasan.

———, 1972, *Philosophy of Mahimā Dharma*, Bhubaneswar: Bhagiratha Prakasan.

———, 1997, *Bhīmā Bhoi: The Adivasi Poet Philosopher*, Bhubaneswar: Bhagiratha Prakasan.

Panda, D. (ed.), 1972, *Mahimā Dharma and Darsan*, Koraput: D.A.V. Colllege.

Panigrahi, S.C., 1998, *Bhīmā Bhoi and Mahimā Darsan*, Bhubaneswar: Deptt. of Philosophy.

Patnaik, Tandra, 2005, *Śūnya-Puruṣa: Bauddha Vaiṣṇavism of Orissa*, Bhubaneswar: Utkal Studies in Philosophy, vol. XII, New Delhi: D.K. Printworld.

Pfeffer, G., 2007, *Periphery and the Centre: Studies in Orissan History, Religion and Anthroplogy*, New Delhi: Manohar.

Satpathy, Siddhartha, 2006, *Prayers and Reflections: Selections from Stutichintamani*, Bhubaneswar: Rupantar.

Senapati, Nilamani, 1975, *Satya Mahimā Dharma*, Cuttack: Dharma Grantha Store.

Singh, Nikky-Guninder Kaur, 1981, *Physics and Metaphysics of the Guru Granth Sahib*, New Delhi: Sterling.

Vasu, N.N., 1911, *Modern Buddhism and Its Followers in Orissa*, Calcutta: Hare Press, repr. Delhi: Gian Publishing House, 1986.

PAPERS (ENGLISH)

Bannerjee, K., 1961, *The Philosophy of Gorakhanath*, Gorakhpur, Mahanta Digvijayanatha Trust.

Banerjee-Dube, Ishita, 1993 (unpublished), "Of Poets and Texts: Bhīmā Bhoi and Mahimā, Religion and Society in Orissa: Mahimā Dharma in Ninteenth and Twentieth Centuries", Calcutta, PhD Dissertation.

———, 1999, "Taming Traditions: Legalities and Histories in 20th Century Orissa", in B. Bhadra (ed.) *Subaltern Studies X: Writings on South Asian History and Society*, New Delhi: Oxford University Press.

———, 2001, "Issues of Faith, Enactment of Contest: The Founding of Mahimā Dharma in 19th Century Orissa", in S. Kulke (ed.) *Jagannath Revisited*, New Delhi: Manohar.

Banerjee-Dube, Ishita and Johannes Beltz, 2008, *Popular Religion and Ascetic Practices: New Studies in Mahima Dharma*, New Delhi: Manohar Publishers.

Beltz, Johannes, 2007, "Contested Authorities, Disputed Centers and Rejected Norms: Situating Mahimā Dharma in its Regional Diversity", in Georg Pfeffr (ed.) *Periphery and Center, Studies in Orissan History and Religion and Anthropology*, New Delhi: Manohar Publishers.

———, 2003, "Bhīmā Bhoi: The Making of a Modern Saint", in A. Copley (ed.) *Hinduism in Public and Private*, Delhi: Oxford University Press.

Das, Cittaranan, 1951, "Studies in Medieval Religion and Literature of Orissa", *Visvabharati Annals*, 3.

Eschmann, A., 1975, "Spread: Organisation, and Cult of Mahimā Dharma", in Nilamani Senapati (ed.) *Mahimā Dharma*, Cuttack: Dharma Grantha Store.

———, 1978, "Mahimā Dharma: An Autochthonous Hindu Reform Movement", in A. Eschmann et al. (eds.) *The Cult of Jagannath and the Regional Tradition of Orissa*, New Delhi: Manohar.

Guzy, Lidia J., 2007, "Negative Estacy or the Singers of the Divine: Voices from the Periphery of Mahimā Dharma", *Periphery and Center: Studies in Orissan History and Religion and Anthropology*, Georg Pfeffer (ed.), New Delhi: Manohar.

Kar, B., 1969, "Religious Philosophy and Mahimā Gosain and his School", *Bharati*, Utkala Journal of Humanities, vol. III.

———, 1972, "Biswanath Bābā on Mahimā and Advaita", *Mahimā Dharma and Darsan*, Daitary Panda (ed.), Koraput.

———, "Biswanatha Bābā and Visuddhadvaita Darsana", *Studies in Mahimā Dharma*, Ishita Banerjee-Dube and Johanne Beltz (eds.).

Mansingh, M., 1982, "The Unique Alekha Cult", in *The Saga of the Land of Jagannātha*, Cuttack: J. Mohapatra Stores.

———, 2003, "Mahimā Dharma Ascetic: A Case Study on Popular Asceticism and its Patronage Structure in Rural Orissa", A. Copley (ed.) *Hinduism in Public and Private*, Delhi: Oxford University Press.

Misra, G., 1972, 'Directorial Introduction to the book' *Mahimā Dharma and Darsan*, ed. D. Panda, Koraput: D.A.V. Colllege.

Index